William Mangam Lawrence

The ideal prayer meeting

Hints and helps towards its realization

William Mangam Lawrence

The ideal prayer meeting
Hints and helps towards its realization

ISBN/EAN: 9783337283704

Printed in Europe, USA, Canada, Australia, Japan

Cover: Foto ©Lupo / pixelio.de

More available books at **www.hansebooks.com**

THE
IDEAL PRAYER MEETING

HINTS AND HELPS TOWARDS ITS REALIZATION

By W. H. GROAT

With Introduction by
Rev. William M. Lawrence, D. D.

"Whatsoever ye do, do it heartily as to the Lord and not unto men"

FLEMING H. REVELL COMPANY
CHICAGO : : NEW YORK : : TORONTO
Publishers of Evangelical Literature

PREFACE.

No meeting of the church should receive more careful consideration and planning than the prayer meeting, even though there be more than one prayer meeting in the church during the week.

Many articles have been written, addresses delivered, and volumes published on nearly every phase of religous life, work and duty, but the one theme that is scarcely less important than the others, viz., the prayer meeting, has received but little attention.

If the prayer meeting is poorly attended and the interest uncertain, all the addresses and newspaper articles that may be heard or read regarding our duty or our interest in the church and its work, will not suffice to arouse the latent energies of the people. If the prayer meeting be well attended and much interest be manifested, the church will surely be in a spiritual condition and results are sure to follow, while if the prayer meeting be not supported, it will surely have an opposite effect.

The writer in preparing for a place to which he had been assigned in a religious gathering, having special reference to the prayer meeting, was considerably surprised to find that but one or two works had yet appeared on the subject. Probably the most helpful book published is that by the late Rev. Lewis O. Thompson, issued by the publishers of this volume. A few ideas contained in that work have been suggestive of some of the thoughts contained in this volume of which due acknowledgement is hereby made.

The aim sought has been to prepare, in as brief form as possible, such suggestions, topics, etc., as would be helpful to leaders, committees or persons having the prayer meeting in charge; also to those participating in the meeting, having in mind the needs of the various religious organizations of both old and young people.

In sending forth this little volume, with considerable misgiving as to its reception and use, the writer, with no pretensions to literary ability, but with a great desire to assist in the Master's service wherever possible, trusts that it may be instrumental in reviving new interest, new enthusiasm, and new inspiration in the prayer meeting.

While adopting as a title "The Ideal Prayer Meeting" the author by no means intends to imply that he has been able to portray such a model, but, as suggested by the sub-title, aims to give a few hints and helps toward its realization.   WM. H. GROAT.

Chicago, June 15th, 1896.

INTRODUCTION.

OF all the duties and privileges that fall to minister or layman there is none requiring more ability than leading the prayer meeting. To select suitable topics is equivalent to forming an accurate judgment regarding the spiritual condition of the church. To induce the people to prepare themselves upon the topics assigned, requires the exercise of the greatest tact and patience. To prepare one's self to lead the meeting demands study quite as careful as that required for the pulpit. It is an art, wherein there is the largest opportunity for failure; and this failure is of the most serious sort, because not only does it concern the welfare of the leader but that of the worshippers. To evoke the spirit of worship, to arouse such an interest that all present shall feel themselves in some sense participants in the privileges of the prayer meeting, and so to conduct the whole service that the meeting shall close upon a higher plane than that which it occupied at its opening, this is the business of the leader.

The author of this book, Mr. Groat, has manifested rare fitness in this capacity and the suggestions which he sets forth in the volume are the results of much practical experience both in his own church and elsewhere.

The suggestions, it will be seen, have a special reference to young people's societies and are designed for the cultivation of the devotional spirit. They are written by one who is himself reverent in his disposition, yet with all they manifest the joyous side of Christian life. They are suggestive. No one can make use of the contents of the volume without enlarging the hints herein offered. They are valuable especially in that they require the constant and careful use of the Bible. They are serious—but not heavy in tone. One of the dangers threatening the prayer meeting is flippancy. The endeavor to get everybody to take part and to define the usefulness and success of a meeting by the number of people actually taking part, results surely in producing a frivolous spirit.

The real prayer meeting is communing together with God and communicating to each other spiritual experiences and invoking together God's blessing and guidance and thereby effecting real consecration. It ought to be the most popular of all the services of the church. To this end the volume is sent forth The author of the book has been prominently known in connection with the work of the young people. He is himself a young man, and is a member of the church of which the writer of this introduction is pastor. The book is sent out by him as his contribution toward the great work of preparing young people for Christian service. It will be found helpful to all, pastors or laymen, who have to meet the responsibility of arranging for prayer meeting. God bless this effort and make it of value to those for whom it is designed.

WILLIAM M. LAWRENCE.

Chicago, June 15th, 1896.

CONTENTS.

		PAGE
	Preface	3
	Introduction	7
I.	The Importance and Purpose of the Prayer Meeting	11
II.	Pastoral Influence and Care	16
III.	Relation of the Prayer Meeting to the Home and Church	19
IV.	Scriptural Hints, References and Suggestions to the Prayer Meeting	22
V.	Requirements for a Successful Prayer Meeting	29
VI.	Equipment	33
VII.	Hindrances to Successful Prayer Meetings	36
VIII.	Attendance	44
IX.	Incentives for Attendance	47
X.	Methods of Conduct	52
XI.	The Transaction of Business in the Prayer Meeting	57
XII.	Time and Place of Holding	60
XIII.	Leaders	65
XIV.	Subjects	75
XV.	Music	79
XVI.	Participation by Members	83
XVII.	A Model Prayer Meeting	90
XVIII.	Committee Work	93
XIX.	Topics and Analyses	95
XX.	Questions Answered	108
XXI.	General Suggestions	114

I.

THE IMPORTANCE AND PURPOSE OF THE PRAYER MEETING.

Our regard for the prayer meeting *away from it*, the interest that we show *in it*, the manner in which we speak *of it*, and our attendance *upon it*, are very sure indications of Christian character. It is possible for the Christian to do without the prayer meeting as it is possible for a child to do without milk, but both are highly necessary for growth; the one for physical and the other for spiritual reasons.

Earnest, zealous, devoted Christians take great delight in the weekly gatherings for prayer and praise, feel strengthened, encouraged and better equipped to meet the difficulties and emergencies of life. To such no persuasion is necessary to enlist their support or attendance. They feel it not only their duty to be present but are anxious to be there.

To other Christians the prayer meeting seems to hold forth no special requirement for their presence, and it is to them a matter of convenience or some unusual attraction if they do attend. There is possibly an explanation for this indifference or lack of interest on the part of many Christians. One person will attend school, become deeply attached to his studies and to the school, and graduate with honors, while another will manage to get through and pass the same assigned studies and lectures mechanically and have little or no interest in the work. But wherein is the difference? Both have attended the same school, had the same teacher and the same studies, and yet there is a marked contrast in their school life and its results. Three elements entered into one student's life that were not in the other: First, a devotion to his work; second, a desire to succeed; third, a sense of duty he owed to himself and his friends.

What is true of school life is also true of religious life. We should always be learning, seeking to know of God's Word and Work.

The prayer meeting is the school of instruction and guidance in Christian life. We shall make slow progress as Christians unless we are devoted to Christ, our instructor and guide; unless we have a desire to serve Him and learn of Him; and unless we feel that we have a duty that we owe to Him, to His cause and to our brethren. And where can we better give expression to these essentials than in the prayer meeting? If we have an inclination to serve Christ only when it does not interfere with our conveniences and desires, if we assemble with our brethren only when duty demands or our conscience prompts, then the prayer meeting has little, if any, significance to us, and our attitude will not be without its deterring influence upon others.

The condition of the prayer meeting is a very sure indication of the spiritual atmosphere and condition of the church. If the prayer meeting is well attended, if there is a constant interest felt in its gatherings, and the meetings are thoroughly pervaded with spirituality, earnest prayers and inspiring songs, the church is sure to thrive and enlarge its field of usefulness; but a dull and lifeless prayer meeting begets the same spirit in other departments of the church, and it is a difficult matter to avoid ensuing hurtful consequences.

The prayer meeting should stand for the Christian as a beacon light of hope, whither he should turn with his conflicts, his doubts and his troubles; and by the fellowship of his brethren, by hearing of their victories, their hope and trust, thank God for the way he has hitherto been led and take fresh courage. Do not understand that the prayer meeting is the place for each to give a recital of all his troubles at home, in business or in society. If this were so one would become a stumbling block in the way of others accepting Christ. by giving the impression that the Christian life is one of trial and tribulation rather than one of joy and peace. When we feel that we specially need the sympathy and encouragement of our brethren to strengthen our faith, no better place than the prayer meeting can be found.

Let the prayer meeting be the place not only where we meet our brethren but where we meet God and receive of His Spirit and of His Word, thus gaining strength to overcome difficulties. If we have been instrumental in leading a soul to Christ, let us tell it. If we have helped some one in the Christian life who has been backsliding, let us speak of it. If we are troubled as to certain passages in God's Word that are not clear to us and wish to know their meaning, let us speak of them. If we know those who are suffering, who are in need of our assistance, or who need our sympathy, let us tell about it, and it will give an opportunity for others to do something for Christ, and will make the prayer meeting a means of usefulness in the church.

The prayer meeting was never intended for the benefit of the pastor or leader alone. It is THE meeting, and the only one, where young and old alike have opportunity to indicate the development of their Christian life, experience and utterance. It is often the only gathering in the week, excepting on the Lord's Day, when members come together; and hence it should also be an opportunity for extending wider acquaintance with one another and enlarging the disposition for sociability within and without the church.

To those outside the church, our regular or irregular attendance at the prayer meeting, in a large measure, indicates our interest in religious things. It is through the prayer meeting that we should receive encouragement for engaging in religious work at home and abroad. Through its influence we should be awakened to the needs about us; to the various evils that we should by voice, by pen, or by ballot, seek to efface.

If the prayer meeting has been to us a meaningless gathering; an occasion where we were to listen throughout an evening to a set address of the pastor or leader on the "Lost Ten Tribes," or kindred topics; if it has been, a gathering for the relation of family troubles or hardships—a meeting where a few constantly take up the time and tell the same story with the change of a few synonymous words; then let us by a determined effort on our part, by personal example and persuasion, seek to infuse into it new life, new zeal, and consecration. And following the example of the early disciples, we shall certainly have history repeating itself—*the Lord adding to the church daily such as should be saved.*

II.
PASTORAL INFLUENCE AND CARE.

In a large number of our churches the pastor leads all the prayer meetings. This is usually the case in churches of limited membership located in the country or in our smaller towns or villages. In larger towns and cities it has been the custom for several years for the pastor to lead the church prayer meeting (both for the old and young people) and some of the members to lead the Mission Band prayer meeting, Christian Endeavor, Baptist Young People's Union, Epworth League, or such other gatherings as are attended more particularly by the young people.

Here it is proposed to consider the pastor's influence and care of the prayer meetings, whether as leader or only in pastoral relation to the meetings. As leader of the prayer meeting the pastor can discover weakness, improper application of Bible truths, lack of growth in his members; and can watch for opportunity to correct, advise or help. He has an opportunity to come closer to his members, to see their individual needs; and to show his interest, not only in their spiritual but also in their temporal trials and difficulties. He uses the prayer meeting to give definite explanation of Bible truths and doctrines in a familiar manner, devoid of the restraint that usually exists between the pulpit and the pew.

If the meeting is in charge of other persons, the pastor drops in at the beginning or close of the meeting to leave some timely thought or suggestion helpful to a better understanding of the topic under discussion. Sometimes it is wise for the pastor to use a portion of the meeting to call attention to some great need or work that ought to be done by the young people or other members of his church. He will usually find it not a difficult matter to shape his thought as an application or a suggestion growing out of the subject of the meeting.

It is not wise for the pastor to come in upon a meeting and without warning discuss some topic or line of work foreign to the one under consideration. Interruptions of this character, if frequent, will undo much of the work of the committee or persons having the meeting in charge.

The pastor will find occasion at times to suggest topics for discussion; objects or occasions for prayer; those who should be called upon to act as leaders; and changes, if any, that should be made in the conduct of the meeting.

To this meeting the pastor will come with words of encouragement to young members, helpful suggestions to those engaged in work, a hearty handshake and a good word for those who are indifferent or timid in taking part in the meeting.

The pastor should be careful not to occupy too much of the time of the meeting but in the broadest manner possible let it be one for the special benefit of the people.

Sometimes it is wise for the pastor to take entire charge of the Young People's Meetings for a time and use them as a means for special instruction in the doctrines or ordinances of the church. If in the case of those attending them there is a special need of such information, it will be better to give up the prayer meeting for a time and acquire the knowledge that will help in the future work of the church.

III.

THE RELATION OF THE PRAYER MEETING TO THE HOME AND THE CHURCH.

Probably no organization, religious or secular, has maintained more closely the same methods of conduct for as long a period as has the church. In fact, we have become so accustomed to the methods in vogue in the school, in the church service, and in the prayer meeting, as to almost know what will be said and done at each of these gatherings without taking the trouble to attend. One of the hopeful signs of the growth and enlargement of the church, in all its various departments, is the progress that has been made in the past two or three years. The new ideas and new enthusiasm that have arisen through associations, conventions, or local gatherings, have not lost to the church its power or its adherence to the truths upon which it is founded, but have aroused new motives, new desires, and new ideas of the duties and privileges of the church, and what the church can and may do.

What is true regarding the church proper is also true regarding the prayer meeting. This meeting has too often been a place of assembly where two or three told their troubles, gave long expositions of Bible doctrines, and where a few hymns were sung in the "old fashioned" way. We are outgrowing these methods in our day. The prayer meeting is helpful to the Christian's home life, and is the one place where evidences of it should certainly be manifested.

Have we laid aside a loved one in the family? Seek fellowship and sympathy in the prayer meeting. We share our mutual woes. Why not there? Do we feel our need of better knowledge of God's Word? The prayer meeting should assist in developing that knowledge. Have our children grown up around us and not accepted Christ? Bring them to the prayer meeting and ask God to direct the meeting to that end. Tell the pastor or leader your desire so that he may co-operate. Is our daily life at home or in business beset with temptations and difficulties? Let the prayer meeting be the connecting link between the Sabbaths to help and strengthen us.

The prayer meeting should be a source of encouragement to the Christian in daily life, furnishing religious information, and aiding in a daily cultivation of piety at home and away from home. While the prayer meeting is, or should be, a help to the Christian in the different places where he may be placed, it is also of the greatest benefit to the church. It should help to equip workers for the Sunday-school, for young people's organizations, or other service. It should help to impress religious truths taught from the pulpit, and serve as an adjunct to it. It should be the avenue through which the pastor reaches his people either by his own ministrations or in connection with those who lead the meetings, as well as an opportunity to reach the unconverted and hold conversation with them at the close of the meetings. The faith, and the unswerving devotion of other Christians, shown in their testimony and in their prayers, will help to strengthen younger or weaker Christians.

The prayer meeting offers the best possible opportunity for church members to become acquainted with one another and to know about the work which is being done, or which needs to be done. If we support the prayer meeting it will help us, and help our brethren also.

IV.

SCRIPTURAL HINTS, REFERENCES AND SUGGESTIONS REGARDING THE PRAYER MEETING.

God's Word contains a great many references relating to the assembling together of Christians for prayer and praise. While a majority of these instances obviously refer to public worship or regular church services, their direct connection with the people and their participation in these gatherings, will doubtless place them on similar footing with our prayer meeting gatherings. A careful reading of the different Biblical references to the people meeting for prayer, for praise to God, for confession, for acknowledgment of His mercies, together with the many exhortations regarding these assemblages, will often be helpful as well as suggestive of some of our weaknesses, and of our need of re consecration and revival in this line of church work.

The Psalmist says: " Let the people praise thee, O God, let all the people praise thee," and again, "I will praise the Lord with my whole heart in the assembly of the upright and in the congregation."

In the Epistles of Paul to the different churches, notice his many exhortations as to their meetings: "Praying always with all prayer and supplication in the Spirit, and watching thereunto with all perseverance and supplication for all saints." Eph. 6:18. "Continue in prayer and watch in the same with thanksgiving." Col. 4:2. "I will therefore that men pray everywhere, lifting up holy hands without wrath and doubting." 1 Tim. 2:8.

Note the words of Christ, "Watch and pray, that ye enter not into temptation." Matt. 26:41 And again, "If two of you shall agree on earth as touching anything that they shall ask, it shall be done for them of my Father which is in heaven. For where two or three are gathered together in my name, there am I in the midst of them." Matt. 18:19 and 20.

Let us note a few of the many references to prayer gatherings spoken of in both the Old and the New Testaments:

Neh. 9:3: "The children of Israel are gathered together for fasting, for confession of their sins and repentance," and we read that "they stood up in their place and read in the Book of the Law of the Lord their God, one fourth part of the day, and another fourth part they confessed and worshipped the Lord their God."

Psalms 65: 1-2: "Praise waiteth for thee, O God in Zion, and unto thee shall the vow be performed, O thou that hearest prayer, unto thee shall all flesh come."

Isa. 56: 7: "For mine house shall be called an house of prayer for all people."

The early church furnished us with several instances of coming together for prayer and praise:

Acts 1: 14: "These all continued with one accord in prayer and supplication with the women and Mary, the mother of Jesus, and with his brethren."

Acts 2: 46-47: "And they continuing daily with one accord in the temple and breaking bread—praising God and having favor with all the people." Note the result—"And the Lord added to the church daily such as should be saved." Acts 12: 5: "Peter therefore was kept in prison, but prayer was made without ceasing of the church unto God for him." Notice 12th verse, same chapter: "He came to the house of Mary the mother of John—where many were gathered together praying."

Acts 13: 3: "And when they had fasted and prayed, and laid their hands on them, (Paul and Barnabas), they sent them away."

Acts 20: 36: "And when he had thus spoken

he (Paul) kneeled down and prayed with them all."

Acts 21:5: "And they all brought us on our way with wives and children till we were out of the city, and we kneeled down on the shore and prayed."

When we read these and other records of early Christian faithfulness in the declaration of Gospel truth, the struggles and trials the early church had to contend with, surely such gatherings for praise, for outpouring of hearts to God in prayer, must have been to all seasons of greatest blessing and nearness to the Master. Can we not emulate the example and endeavor to have like gatherings? We no doubt have many such meetings, where we are brought to feel our nearness to Christ; and it is these gatherings from which ascend the prayers of the saints, which we are told (Rev. 8: 3-4) are offered upon the golden altar before the throne.

We have glanced at some features of the gatherings for prayer mentioned in the Bible. Let us also look at a few references to individual testimony and prayer, and we shall surely be impressed with the directness of the testimony of Christ's disciples concerning Him:

Peter: "Thou art the Christ, the Son of the Living God."

Thomas: "My Lord and my God."

The Centurion: "Truly this was the Son of God."

But all testimonies were not as direct and pointed as were these; some were more lengthy. Peter on the Day of Pentecost has twenty-three verses of testimony recorded, two of exhortation, and other words unrecorded. Stephen before the Council has fifty-two verses, and Paul before Agrippa has twenty-six verses of testimony.

In these days when time is valuable, when we are progessing along all lines of thought and action, we have not the time in our prayer meetings for many exhortations like Paul's, Stephen's, or Peter's; what we want is conclusive evidence of "Christ in us, the hope of glory," earnest, helpful thoughts, delivered after the manner and spirit of these early disciples.

But a prayer meeting without prayer, is as vacant as a tenantless house. Notice the individual prayers of the Bible, and the various differences in their brevity and their accomplishment.

Long Prayers: Solomon's (Dedication of the Temple), 2 Chron. 6: 14-42.
Our Savior's (for the disciples), John 17: 1-26.
The Lord's Prayer for His disciples (for every requisite), Matt. 6: 9-13.

Short Prayers: The Publican—"Lord be merciful to me a sinner." Luke 18:13.
Peter—"Lord save me." Matt. 14:30.
The Lepers — "Jesus, Master, have mercy on us." Luke 17:13.

Very Earnest Prayers:
Elijah before the prophets of Baal. 1 Kings 18:36-37.
Abraham for Sodom. Gen. 18:23-32.
Blind Bartimeus. Mark 10:47.

Answered Prayers:
The Thief on the Cross. Luke 23:42-43.
Elijah, for the widow's son. 1 Kings 17:21-22.
The Church, for Peter. Acts 12:5, 11.

Unanswered Prayers:
Zebedee's wife. Matt. 20:21.
The Pharisee. Luke 18:11-12.
Jonah. Jonah 4:2-3.

We have then a number of different methods for bringing requests to God in prayer. We can learn one truth in connection with this study, if it may be so termed,—that earnest, heartfelt prayer to God for a definite purpose or object, whether long or brief, he will surely answer.

We cannot probably emphasize the matter better, in concluding this topic, than to call attention to the words of Christ: "Whosoever, therefore, shall confess me before men, him will I confess also before my Father which is in heaven." Matt. 10:32. And the words of Paul in 1 Cor. 14:15: "I will pray with the spirit and I will pray with the understanding also; I will sing with the spirit and I will sing with the understanding also." Again in the 26th verse: "How is it then, brethren? When ye come together every one of you hath a psalm, hath a doctrine, hath a tongue, hath a revelation, hath an interpretation. Let all things be done unto edifying."

40th verse: "Let all things be done decently and in order."

V.
REQUIREMENTS FOR A SUCCESSFUL PRAYER MEETING.

The first requirement for a successful prayer meeting is attendance. If the attendance is uncertain, or if those who have influence in the church fail to support it, then seeking to continue the interest is uphill work.

The meeting should contain sympathetic and responsive Christians—those who have a purpose in attending and who reflect the benefit they receive afterwards. If we attend simply because the night set is convenient, and it is our custom to do so, or because it is expected of us, or that we may adjust some items of business either before or after meeting, arrange social calls, or avoid other gatherings where expense would be incurred, we have set a very low standard of our value of the prayer meeting. Let us have a motive and purpose that prompts us to attend what should be a means of grace, and let that purpose be in keeping with the service that we seek and that we need.

The prayer meeting should be as its name

implies, a place for prayer, whether silent or audible prayer. To hold prayer meetings without prayer is like trying to run a locomotive without fuel. The leader should be prepared. It may be possible here and there for a leader to give an interesting and practical talk without preparation, but there are few leaders so far advanced or of so great capability as not to find that a little preparation will make their remarks still more forcible and better appreciated.

The music should be whole-souled and inspiring. Songs or hymns should be sung that are familiar or that are productive of devotion and praise to God.

The testimonies should indicate some originality of thought or study, not stereotyped utterances or remarks copied from others; then, if judicious and wisely developed, they will be helpful.

The participation should be voluntary and not forced or requested. It will thus have greater value and will be more helpful to those who are timid and fearful. Preparation should be made before coming to the meeting, so that one may be ready when opportunity offers. Timely suggestions, well considered, will be helpful to the meeting.

Every feature of the meeting should be conducted with promptness—the beginning, the singing, the leader's remarks, participation by mem-

REQUIREMENTS FOR SUCCESSFUL MEETING 31

bers, and the time of closing meeting. If the prayer meeting is to be a continued success, there should be evidences of growth in interest, in attendance, progress made in Bible knowledge, and in the readiness and ability of those who attend to take part in the meetings. The meetings should be characterized by a deep undercurrent of spirituality, coupled with a desire to reach those who are not Christians. There should be a hearty welcome for strangers and for those who have been direlict in attendance. And for all the brethren or sisters, a genuine, hearty handshaking and much of sociability.

If you have subscribed to a pledge that calls for the fulfilment of some duty when attending the prayer meeting, do not shirk it, but promptly and cheerfully comply; it will help you and assist the meeting.

There should be a place for the pastor in the meeting when he is not the leader. He should be remembered in the prayers of the people that he may have God's presence, His power and His Spirit, to help him in his work.

In addition to the various suggestions offered as to the requirements for successful prayer meetings, as well as to many others that have not been mentioned, there is one element that is not required, and that is criticism. This is the weapon that has helped to kill more prayer meetings than any other: The pastor talks too long or is too prosy. Brother A has a nasal twang. Sister B is too melancholy. Sister C does not use good grammar. Music is not just right, etc., etc. If you find these various faults, take them home with you and bury them; in any case, don't speak of them to others. If someone calls your attention to these faults, change the subject and speak of some things that are helpful and good. See what you can do to prevent these difficulties and avoid their recurrence. Remember the Master's words: "Judge not that ye be not judged."

VI.
EQUIPMENT.

In order that any organization may be managed successfully, there should be completeness in details and some system in management. An enterprise, religious or otherwise, that is conducted in any other way, can scarcely continue on a permanent basis. This should be characteristic of the church in all its departments. Meetings that are not directly under the pastor's charge, should be taken care of by a vigorous, wide-awake devotional or prayer meeting committee. This committee should be possessed of life without frivolity, originality without unseemly peculiarities, and energy coupled with religious fervor.

The leader should be chosen not alone for the benefit that he may receive, but also for what he can give to others; and hence the leader should be one who will attract people to the meetings and sustain interest in them.

There should be if possible, a chorister or leader of the singing, one who enters into the spirit of the songs, one filled with love for

Christ such as will seek its highest expression in whole-souled music.

Stationed at the door should be two or three ushers to seat the strangers who may come in or those who are necessarily late. They should be capable of giving a hearty welcome to those that come, a warm grasp of the hand, a word of introduction to other members or to the pastor, and, above all, see that all are acquainted and made to feel at home.

There should be a janitor or someone on hand to see that the lecture room or place of meeting is properly aired and ventilated. A dull heavy atmosphere is almost sure to have a depressing effect on the meeting. Bibles should be available for use in every seat and opportunity should always be found for their use. There should also be sufficient singing books, so that there is a book for every one or two persons present. The books should contain hymns that are helpful to the spirit of worship and praise. There should also be cards, slips, calendars or other method of announcing the subjects and the scripture lesson; this will enable those who are timid or require preparation to be ready to take part in the meeting. If there is a chorister or leader, there should also be a musical instrument—cornet, organ or piano—and someone prepared to accompany. The instrument used should be properly tuned and in harmony with the service of song. A bulletin board is also a valuable adjunct to the meeting, and many long announcements of meetings or other matter may be placed there and save time as well as patience. There should also be a clock where it can be seen. When it indicates the hour of opening service, promptly the meeting should begin, and as it strikes or indicates the closing hour, unless in the most exceptional cases, the meeting should close. A small hand-bell will also be serviceable in calling the meeting together at the beginning. Then, last and in nowise of least importance, there should be an attendance of earnest, zealous Christians.

VII.
HINDRANCES TO SUCCESSFUL PRAYER MEETINGS.

Very few prayer meetings, whether of the church proper or of the young people, can be successfully conducted without some obstacles or hindrances arising to interfere with the efforts that are made. The foremost and greatest hindrance is criticism. It does not show itself by public expression in the prayer meeting but by individual comment afterwards. A says to B : What poor singing we had, what a rambling talk the leader gave, what a poor attendance. B meets C and says: The singing in our prayer meeting is "just awful" and the pastor is not a bit interesting any more and attendance is getting smaller. C meets A and says he just feels that the prayer meeting is in a bad way and he has "half a mind not to go again." A, B and C, with their criticisms, each reaching several other members with the same or other criticisms, will cause the general opinion to prevail that the prayer meetings are about ready to fall through. Each one of those who have heard the criticisms is very likely to carry this spirit of failure into the meeting and so the leader is nonplussed at the lack of interest and participation in the meeting, and it is uphill work if indeed the interest in the meeting can be maintained.

Another reason for the lessening of interest in our prayer meetings is their formal and stereotyped character. It is of course expected that in every prayer meeting there should be method in conducting them. No objection ought to be made to meetings being conducted in accordance with some preconceived or well determined plan, but to make these meetings constantly of the same character, with no change of leader, no departure from the old-time songs or from the line of topics usually considered, and having the same number of songs; prayers of the same length and number; the same persons called upon or participating, and using the same general language from meeting to meeting;—the adoption of such methods of procedure cannot fail to hinder the growth of or interest in any prayer meeting. Unprepared leaders are also hurtful to any meeting. It is possible in large churches and especially in those where there are many earnest Christian workers to tide over occasional meetings where the success is entirely dependent on the members. It may be necessary occasionally, for the sake of developing a younger Christian as a leader, or when the person assigned is unable to be present, to use leaders not fully prepared, but for other occasions, if the leaders come unprepared, depending upon circumstances or some sudden inspiration for something to say on the topic assigned, there cannot fail to be a feeling of disappointment on the part of those present in not learning something further than that gained by their own study on the subject.

Unprepared members are also in a measure a hindrance to the successful continuance and growth of prayer meetings. Every Christian should endeavor to have some thought, some suggestion, some plea, some heartfelt desire. purpose or prayer, for every prayer meeting, whether opportunity is offered to speak or not. We can at least prepare ourselves for the meeting by praying for it and for our own and others' help from it.

Unannounced topics is another hindrance, and more especially to younger Christians, and to those who have difficulty in expressing themselves readily in public. To such persons ideas may come in the meetings where the topic has not been previously announced, but the fear of failure, of criticism or of inability to speak as grammatically or as effectually as others, often hinders them from taking any part in the meeting.

Meetings without any plan or method do not readily thrive and develop. If leaders are chosen haphazard, without reference to spirituality, ability or desirability; if topics are selected at random without reference to the needs of the people; if chorister or organist, or both, are secured after arriving at the meeting, or if the singing is conducted without them if they cannot be had; such methods will certainly very materially deprive the meeting of interest and support.

New or unfamiliar hymns are also productive of lack of interest in the meetings. It is well, at certain times, when announcement is duly made, to learn new songs that are suggestive and helpful. If there is considerable musical talent among the young people, it would be well to have them learn new pieces apart from the meeting, and, with their knowledge of them, use them in the meeting at occasional intervals. Music is an important feature of the prayer meeting; but do not spoil it by manifesting a continued desire for something new, simply for the novelty of it.

Long or pedantic prayers help to lessen the interest in the prayer meeting. How many of the prayers that are offered are meaningless! a recital merely of our own doings, or of the weaknesses of others; and yet they are offered before God as prayer. Do we forget what prayer means, through whose name it should be offered, and the reasons why we should pray and the objects we should pray for? The repetition of experiences or cant phrases is another element that hinders the successful prayer meeting. Some years ago we were converted. The experience was of great moment to us; the greatest, possibly, that we have ever had; but why rehearse it over and over again to others; let us get some new experience that will be helpful. By all means let us avoid the many cant religious terms and sayings that are so common, and let us seek, yet with humbleness, for originality in thought and utterance.

Unnatural testimony is another means of injuring the prayer meeting. Giving expression to feelings and requests in a meeting for the sake of making a "good prayer=meeting speech," when there is no sincere desire to enter into the conditions required. Also giving testimony that is beyond our experience or knowledge, but which is common to prayer meeting gatherings, is decidedly hurtful.

Unsociability—coming to the meetings and returning home without seeking to meet new members and strangers, and with very little effort to meet those who are regular members of the church is another hindrance. How often a hearty handshake, a kindly word, or an intro-

HINDRANCES TO SUCCESSFUL MEETINGS 41

duction at the prayer meeting, has been helpful to the meeting and to ourselves.

Personal pride is another barrier to the success of the prayer meeting. It may show itself in our remaining away on account of uncongeniality with those who attend or are accustomed to take part; in not being asked to take the leadership of some of the meetings or fill some prominent place; in not receiving public recognition or mention as others sometimes do.

Lack of interest is not infrequently the principal cause of failure, of small attendance or weak prayer meetings. The occasion for this lack of interest is often due to the methods employed in the conduct of the meetings. But while this may be true in many cases, is it not often that the trouble is with ourselves? If we came to the meetings with a determination to do our part to make them helpful, if we have already prayed for their success, for spirituality, for personal growth in them, and then by our influence help to sustain them, the question of lack of interest would scarcely arise. But it does not happen this way. We come home from business, tired and worried with the day's events, and in this frame of mind go to the prayer meeting; the same feeling has possession of several others, and so the influence is contagious, and the result is a meeting of like character unless a goodly number of others have determined to rise above circumstances and help the meeting to be successful.

Tardiness is also an element that hinders the success of a prayer meeting. If the leader begins the meeting irregularly, instead of at the time appointed, the members invariably come late, feeling that they sustain no loss by so doing. If we are going to take a train we know that we will have to be at the depot at the scheduled hour of departure. When we go to our daily work, having appointed hours for business, we endeavor to be there at that time. Why, then, can we not arrange to be just as prompt in the Lord's sevice and not deprive others of benefits they would have received but for our tardiness?

Absence of leader or chorister is also detrimental to the meeting. When either knows that he will be absent from the next meeting, the fact should be communicated at once to the committee or person in charge of the meeting, so that there may be other arrangements made and the meeting may not suffer thereby. If the leader or chorister plans to go away and advises no one of his intention, and the members come to the meeting with no knowledge of his being absent, a disappointment is very certain to be felt by all, and a few repetitions will cause great injury to the meetings.

Too many and too long notices are very apt to dampen the interest of the meeting. There are some notices that from their nature should be mentioned, but a multiplicity of notices to indicate the many lines of work in which the church is engaged, or read as a means of gratification to some outside party is very unwise—particularly if it is noticed that strangers are present. It is very apt to lead the minds of the people away from such preparation as they may have made on the topic to be considered, and spoil the meeting.

Another hindrance is the continuance of the meetings beyond the time designated. This sometimes happens when it has been found at the close of the meeting that the disposition to take part has been aroused and there seems to be a "crowding" of one another to take part. Then some leaders continue the meeting until all who desired have participated, thereby prolonging it unduly. If this is taken as an indication of the wisdom of overrunning the time of the meeting, future meetings will disclose the folly of so doing. Because an article of food or fruit is pleasant to the taste, it does not become us to eat until we can do so no longer—we are apt to lose our desire for it; but if we eat a reasonable quantity and then leave it with a desire for more, next time we shall still be fond of the article. If the prayer meeting is of great interest at the close, better stop and leave a desire for more than to continue until all are satisfied and even tired

VIII.
ATTENDANCE.

One fact in connection with the attendance at the prayer meeting should be recognized at the outset, and that is that we cannot expect to have all the members present at all the meetings. These conditions are not entirely due to neglect, to lukewarmness, or to lack of interest. In glancing over our records of attendance (if they are kept) or in noting from week to week the number present, we are apt to feel discouraged, and perhaps to find fault, on account of absentees; when for good reasons, it is not possible for them to be there. Some are obliged to work nights, some to remain at home that other members of the family may have opportunity to go out, some again may be detained at home by sickness or by lack of someone to accompany them to the place of meeting. Especially is this true in the case of girls or young ladies who have long distances to go to the meetings. These and many similar excuses are reasonable and proper, but not all who are absent are detained for reasons of this kind. In some cases, special gatherings, concerts or lectures elsewhere, a social call here or there is the cause of absence from meeting. Or, perhaps, a tired, listless feeling comes over one and he says that the meeting can get along without him and so stays at home. It is this class of uncertain attendants that calls for much thought on the part of those who have the care of the prayer meetings. How shall we divert their attention or secure their interest? How shall we reach them? That is the problem.

Members who are irregular in their attendance or who have ceased to have interest, should be encouraged by visits from other members (especially of those who will be judicious and sociable) and by officers of the church or local society, or by a kindly letter from the Lookout or Membership Committee.

In this connection the roll-call in young peoples societies will be found especially of service. Attention being directed to absentees by failure to respond to roll-call should be noted by other members, and they should be promptly sought after and urged to be present at future meetings.

In some cases, possibly, members have been frightened by the fear of their being called on unexpectedly to take part in the meetings, and feeling that they are not prepared or unable to do so, have stayed away. Great care should be taken in our zealousness not to be too anxious to have inexperienced members take part or we may drive them from us.

In the prayer gathering, members should be made to feel that this is the meeting in which they are interested and it is *their* meeting. It is the meeting for their development in spiritual things. If they adopt an idea of this kind, they will make an effort to be present whenever possible.

In addition to those who attend the weekly gatherings for prayer, we should look for the faces of others than our own membership. Individually we should seek out those who do not attend such a service, make an appointment with and have them accompany us to the meeting. We should make an effort to bring to the service those who are not Christians, and seek to get them interested in their souls' salvation; thus making the meeting the gateway to the church.

IX.
INCENTIVES TO ATTENDANCE.

One feature that has as much to do with the success of the prayer meeting as any other, is the music. There should be vigorous, inspiring music. A whole-souled, earnest leader, who enters into the spirit of the songs and sings himself with much force and power, will be the means of stirring up others to do so; and good music will encourage attendance at the meetings.

Another feature, and of no less importance, is the testimonies given. If those who take part endeavor to make their testimonies pointed and brief, seek to give expression to original thoughts and suggestions, put their own individuality into what they say, avoiding the opposite extreme of "crankism," every testimony made will have earnest listeners, and each person present will obtain a benefit.

Prayer is and should always continue to be the Christian's strength and support. A meeting conducted without prayer is like a dinner-table without meat, a factory without power, a wagon without a horse. The prayer meeting to be what its name implies should have frequent prayers, earnest, brief, and for a purpose. A child would not come to a parent seeking something from him and expect to have his request granted by merely telling where he had been, what he was going to do, and what mistakes he had made. As a matter of information or merely in the way of conversation he might tell this before or after his request, but if he wanted something, he would directly ask for it and would not multiply words in doing so unless it was something far beyond his expectation and he wished to make his need more clear and explicit. God is our father; when we come to Him let us come to Him in like manner in faith, believing that we shall receive. "And this is the confidence that we have in him that if we ask anything according to his will, he heareth us, and if we know that he heareth us, we know that we have the petitions that we desired of him."

If a topic or line of thought has been designated for the meeting in order that those who attend may be interested, not only for that meeting but for the future, the topic should be closely followed by the leader as well as by those participating. Unless an effort is made to keep the thought of the meeting running along one channel, the possibilities are that it will drift into so many different lines as to weaken the interest otherwise shown.

There is nothing so helpful or so restful in whatever connection it may be found as variation or change. We may find here and there examples of persons who have lived for many years in one location, who have never gone any distance from home, who have no knowledge of the scenery, the developments, the great things that have been achieved or are in progress in other places. But such people are few in number. To most individuals there is a desire to get away occasionally from home scenes, to learn what other people are doing; and though one may come home satisfied that he has not learned much, yet the change has been a benefit and a relief for the time being and gives fresh strength for work in the future.

We recognize this same principle in our daily food; whether by stress of circumstances, by physician's suggestion or by unforseen conditions, we are obliged to maintain the same articles of food for successive days, we are very apt to become tired of them and crave something different. Possibly something less wholesome may be offered but it is nevertheless acceptable as a change of diet. In a general sense this is true of most articles of food excepting such staple articles as bread and potatoes. What is true of our food, of our change of location for a time, is also true, in a measure, of the prayer meeting. Singing and prayer, (more particularly, prayer,) are the standard features of the meeting and cannot be dispensed with. Other changes, variations in the conduct of the exercises; in the topics, and in the methods of presenting them; will with changes in leaders be an incentive for attendance upon the meetings.

If the prayer meeting is a source of information in devotional or general religious knowledge; a help to the teacher in the Sunday-school, to the worker in other departments of the church; if it causes spiritual development and helps in other ways, it is certainly the one place attendance at which ought not to require special urging, but we should feel that its benefits demanded our regular presence.

If the prayer meeting is a place not only for receiving suggestions and helps for our work, but also a place where reports are made of work that has been attempted (possibly the work has not been successful, if so, the probable reasons may be discussed), such indications of activity in the church will be a source of inspiration to others who are timid or not doing work, and it may be the means of securing not only their attendance but arouse them to work.

Probably the one feature that has as great a bearing on the prayer meeting attendance as any other, is sociability. It is no more possible to have a live, earnest, wideawake prayer meeting where members shake hands by their finger tips and bow in a cold, formal way, than it is to have an enjoyable evening sitting alone in a room on a cold night without any fire. If we have a bank account, servants to wait on us, and a carriage at our command; when we meet poor Brother B., with his meagre income and a struggling existence, if we give him a hearty handshake it will be a great help to him. Let us lay aside our social prejudices, our political diferences, our position in public life, our differences in temporal life; and when we gather together in God's House, all members of His family, fellow citizens of the household of saints, let us seek to come near to Him and help one another. If the attendance and interest of the prayer meeting increase, it is an indication of permanent growth and continued success. To this end we should labor and pray, and gratifying results will be sure to follow.

X.
METHODS OF CONDUCT.

Every gathering, without regard to its origin or purpose, must needs have some distinctive underlying principles by which it is controlled and directed. The city or town council meetings are conducted in accordance with the resolutions that may be presented in the petitions or by the statements of the representatives of the city. Political meetings are conducted upon the principles that are in accord with the party holding the meeting. What is true of secular meetings is also true, in a sense, of prayer meetings. The prayer meeting should be conducted on the principles and in conformity to the teachings of God's Word. While it may be true that the meetings are presided over, and that the methods of conduct are, in a general sense, on much the same basis in the majority of evangelical churches, yet it is not out of place to call attention to some leading characteristic that should be found in all prayer gatherings that are conducted in accordance with Bible principles. This is not a place where personal ambitions are to be gratified, secular measures considered, or the whims or caprices of the pastor or any of the members of the church advocated; neither is it a place for unloading ideas, plans or prospects that are advanced solely for effect or for public recognition. It is the prayer meeting; let it be so in character, in plan and conduct. Keep the prayer meeting out of ruts. The person who is content to have the same articles of food every day, to go to work and return the same way, answer his correspondence or do whatever duty he or she may have to do in the same manner day after day, does not enjoy life to the fullest extent. The monotony of actions of this kind has its effect on every person, so that in course of time he becomes an automatic, living machine. We would not say anything against one being faithful, or being always at his post, though we might say severe things against those who are fickle and inconstant; but what we do need and what the church needs in all her members is life, push, originality of thought, earnestness, consecration, and continuance therein.

The prayer meeting should be conducted with promptness. There is no reason why religious gatherings should not be conducted with as much system, decision and dispatch as commercial or secular enterprises. Because the larger part of the meeting consists of voluntary participation or assistance it should not for a moment be thought that it can be run in a haphazard or uncertain manner. Promptness should characterize every feature of the meeting,—the commencement, leader's remarks, singing, participation and the closing of the meeting. Tardiness or uncertainty as to the conduct of the meeting, is apt to discourage those who are accustomed to regularity and system in the daily conduct of their affairs and lead them to stay away. The prayer meeting should, as a general rule, be conducted along one or two lines. Either it will be voluntary, or what might be designated as stereotyped or formal, or it will be the reverse. Very exceptional cases are those of a medium between the two, as a tendency started along either line is almost certainly destined to develop into a constant meeting of the same type.

With the information that is so readily obtainable along all lines of religious work, and with the growing tendency to encourage and follow systematic plans of Bible study, there can be little reason why most Christian people should not be prepared to take part in our prayer meetings and do so voluntarily. Meetings of the stereotyped kind are fostered by repetitions of old time experiences, by the infrequency of participation of younger Christians, often through a monopoly of the meetings by older Christians, and frequently by those who have nothing of special interest to add to the enlightenment of the meeting, and by a lack of any variation from the methods always in vogue in the conduct of the meetings. If choice were to be made between the two plans of conduct, who would not prefer the former as the more beneficial and likely to promote growth.

The meeting may be conducted by the pastor, by the deacons or elders, or by the members of the church. In smaller towns and villages it is convenient and probably wise for the pastor to assume the leadership, if but one prayer meeting is held during the week. If separation is made between the older and the younger members, it will be wise for the young people to take the leadership of their own meeting and the pastor to take his. The change of leaders gives opportunity to develop members, adds variety to the meetings, and is conducive to more helpful gatherings than under one leadership, unless the leader be a man of more than ordinary educational or spiritual force.

The length of the meetings is another feature that has much to do with their success. They may be continued until everyone who has anything to say or to pray for has been given an opportunity, or they may be concluded when the hour is up, regardless of other speakers. What is true with reference to overeating something that pleases us and the consequent desire to postpone another feast of the same kind for a considerable time, is also true of the prayer meeting. If we had eaten an insufficiency of the article we were fond of, we should not have become so soon tired of it. So if the meeting is closed when there is a tendency to show further interest, the next one will be all the better for it.

The idea of rotation or change of leaders which is being followed by a large majority of our young people's prayer meetings has been a diffcult one to imitate in smaller churches and also in many larger ones where a few come to the front and assume the leadership, for a very large proportion are too timid or backward to lead the meetings. This last difficulty is now being overcome by having two members appointed for the same meeting,—an experienced and an inexperienced member; the inexperienced member announcing the hymns and reading the lesson, while the other speaks on the topic assigned. This will give the younger or inexperienced confidence in taking part, and in course of time fit them to take their places as regular leaders?

Why should not the prayer meeting be a training school for leaders? For who can say what these young or inexperienced leaders may in the future develop?

XI.
THE TRANSACTION OF BUSINESS IN THE PRAYER MEETING.

It frequently happens that in religious gatherings the object for which the people are assembled is lost sight of by the intrusion of matters of business. There are always sure to be some announcements, appointments, or other details in connection with church work, that will require publicity, and necessarily so; but the manner in which they are made public and the time consumed in bringing them before the people, are often the means of breaking the interest in the prayer meetings.

There are three methods by which announcements may be made.

First: By oral announcement. If the pastor or leader makes a brief, concise statement of such matters as are deemed important, without lengthy or unnecessary explanation, loses no time in the conduct of the business, and passes promptly to the religious duties of the meeting, no injury is done and criticism will seldom follow. If announcements could be made just previous to opening the prayer meeting it would be a more desirable plan. In making announcements, care should always be taken not to call attention to meetings in which the people are not interested or to matters that will divert attention from the work in which they are engaged. The wisdom of this suggestion will readily be understood in those churches where young people have a tendency to roam hither and thither when any new movement springs up, and so lose sight of their own work.

Second: By bulletin. Find a prominent place in the church or lecture room and have a good sized bulletin-board made and hung in the place provided, then tack or pin to it all special notices pertaining to the current week, excepting, possibly, regular church appointments. Call attention to the board occasionally, as a reminder that there is something to be found there, and in course of time it will be consulted, and meetings will be remembered fully as well as by public announcement.

Third: By calendar. In many of the larger churches, in recent years, a daily calendar of meetings and events of the week is kept, thereby avoiding loss of time in public announcement at the preaching service. Such an arrangement is available for other departments of the church's work. In young people's societies, notice of the meetings of social, missionary, temperance, lookout or other committees, special meetings, lectures, etc., may be issued in calendar form, weekly, semi-monthly, or monthly. It may be arranged also to include in such announcements the prayer meetings, topics, officers of the society, etc. Matters of business affecting a committee or a society only, should be arranged, if possible, either before or after service, and not brought before all the people, thus taking up their attention and thereby losing much interest to the prayer gathering.

XII.
TIME AND PLACE OF HOLDING.

The time and place of holding prayer meetings usually varies according to the local requirements of the church holding them; but a few suggestions along this line, seemingly trite to some, may be helpful to others.

It frequently happens that a great many Christians are weakest in that which seems to be almost too trite for consideration in religious teachings or religious work generally. The writer in teaching a large class of young people of ages averaging from fifteen to twenty-two, many of whom were members of the church, once asked several of the class how they knew they were Christians. He was astonished at the difficulty in getting a satisfactory answer. And yet this should be the first thing we should be satisfied about after becoming Christians. Bearing in mind Paul's exhortation—"Have a reason for the hope that is within you." So with the prayer meeting, the time and place for holding, seemingly unimportant, may have much to do with its success or failure.

The one principle that should govern the appointment of a place, day and hour of service, should be that of giving the greatest good to the greatest number. No church can successfully be maintained without a prayer meeting, whether of young or old people, or of both, so that if a week night meeting fails to be supported, the prayer meeting should not be given up, but arrangements should be made to hold it on Sunday. This refers, of course, to the smaller and struggling churches. In the larger and more prosperous, prayer meetings are arranged for on both week days and Sundays.

If the meeting is held on Sunday, circumstances will govern the time for calling it. If there be but one preaching service on Sunday, have the prayer meeting in the afternoon; if two, have the meeting before preaching service at night. Aim to have enquirers or unconverted at the meeting, and then take them into the preaching service, thus getting them, if possible, to commit themselves to the service of Christ.

Some churches have an early morning prayer meeting before preaching service, and the meeting has been of great power; others have prayer meeting both before and after preaching service.

The multiplication of services on the Lord's Day for the sake of effect or without good reason for doing so, is apt to load up some willing members with additional burdens too heavy to be borne, or lead to religious dissipation that in the end may be hurtful, and should be guarded against.

The Second Baptist Church of Chicago, of which the writer is a member, has its prayer meetings arranged as follows:

Sunday evening at 6:30 P. M.—Mission Band or Yoke Fellows Prayer Meeting, open to all.

Monday evening, 8:00 P. M. to 9:00 P. M.— Young People's Prayer Meeting.

Wednesday evening, 7:45 P. M. to 9:00 P. M. —General Prayer Meeting of the church.

An additional prayer meeting is usually held during the winter months on Friday evenings, 7:45 to 9:00 P. M. for scholars in the Sunday-school and for those who are attending day-school, and are studying on the other evenings during the week.

This general arrangement has met with success and may be suggestive to other churches in arranging for their meetings.

Another feature that also deserves some consideration is the room in which the meeting is held. A room that is largely out of proportion to the number in attendance, one that is poorly ventilated, either too chilly or too insufferably close, badly lighted, kept in an untidy manner, cannot fail to have a depressing and discouraging effect on those who attend. In some cases where members are banded together, struggling for existence as a church, many of these difficulties have to be encountered; but with a little and united effort some of these evils may be remedied or lessened. The meetings should be held in a room where the people can come close together, as did the disciples in the upper room, and more freedom will certainly result than by separation through many unoccupied seats. The most suitable place for holding the prayer meetings is the church (lecture room or Sunday-school room, if one be provided). Our Lord's recognition of the church, the associations that cluster around it, its separateness from ordinary edifices, make it our first selection for prayer gatherings. Open air prayer meetings are very helpful if held where the people congregate, and when conducted with energy, promptness and prayerfulness. Cottage prayer meetings are also very helpful in the rural districts and among the smaller and weaker churches.

In the summer months some societies discontinue the prayer meetings. While there may be reasons that would seem to justify such a course, yet the writer feels that, notwithstanding some inconveniences as to heat, extra work, absence of members on vacation, etc., as long as there are those who manifest an interest in the prayer meeting and support it, the meeting had better be continued through the vacation season. In doing so, there is this advantage, that instead of being obliged to start out where the connection was dropped at the beginning of the summer months, the meetings may be continued with the interest which has already been shown, and they will develop.

XIII.
LEADERS.

In selecting leaders for the prayer meetings, it would be well for us to bear in mind God's words to Samuel in selecting one of Jesse's sons for king—" Look not on his countenance or the height of his stature, for man looketh on the outward appearance but God looketh on the heart." Do not select leaders on account of personal appearance only, to gratify someone's ambition, or to give someone prominence not obtained in other ways. Selections of this kind are apt to prove disastrous, even though faithful members stand back of the prayer meeting.

There are three elements that should be considered in selecting a leader: Spirituality, ability, and tact.

Spirituality is needed to inculcate a like response from those who attend; ability, in order that something may be learned and all may be benefited; tact, so that unwise interruptions or an unwise drift in the character of the meeting may be properly controlled and not work injury.

Still another feature may enter into our selection, and that is recognition of Christian character or valuable services rendered by one of older years, or one long in the service.

In order that there may be those who are qualified to serve as leaders, there must be preparation—the preparation that is given through the church and that which is acquired by personal efforts and study.

The church offers great facilities for preparing religious workers or leaders for the prayer meeting. Beginning with the holding of office in the Sunday-school and teaching a class, then taking a place in the young people's work, a large number of young people find themselves fitted to lead a prayer meeting satisfactorily. If this preparation does not give leaders sufficient confidence, a topic may be assigned them to be spoken upon in the meeting; afterwards, a small prayer gathering conducted by them will usually be helpful.

But in addition to the preparation that they have had given them, a leader also needs, and should not fail to make, preparation for himself. The first preparation is earnest prayer; second, liberal use of the Bible; third, the aid of a concordance; fourth, outside helps, in the way of religious publications, or anything that will supplement the information already acquired.

Where the prayer meetings are in charge of a committee, or some one designated for that work, there should be an understanding between the leader and the committee or person in charge as to the manner in which meetings are to be conducted. If the meetings are allowed to drift hither and thither at the option of the leader (well qualified or not) without reference to time, to subject matter, or what is expected, it will be only a question of time when someone will enquire why the meetings do not appear to be as well attended or as interesting as formerly. In giving instructions or suggestions to leaders, it would be well to advise them as to the length of their remarks, the special line of thought to be followed in connection with the topic suggested, if any, and the continuance of the meeting.

FORM OF NOTIFICATION.

Mr.......... is requested to lead the (　　　　) meeting on .... evening, ... '94.

The subject will be " .... "

Please note the following suggestions to leaders.

If, for any reason, you are unable to be present on the evening of the meeting, send me prompt notice so that another leader may be provided.

Yours truly,

....
Chairman Devotional Committee.

SUGGESTIONS TO LEADERS.

Preparation.—Think over the subject and reading lesson and endeavor to get a new thought each day.

One or two timely illustrations are apt to render the opening remarks more interesting to younger members.

Make good use of the Bible, in connection with a Concordance first; with other helps afterwards.

Have your subject matter sifted down to practical, inspiring, and helpful thoughts, any one of which will be a subject for further enlargement in the meeting.

If notes are needed for reference, have them arranged so that they may be readily used, and not delay the meeting while trying to find your way out of a difficulty.

Bear in mind you are to lead a service of prayer and worship. Seek to be in harmony with the service you are endeavoring to aid and encourage.

Prayer.—For assistance in understanding God's Word.
For help in expounding The Word.
For results from the meeting.

Promptness.—Begin the meeting promptly.
Close promptly—before, if service is ended.
Be ready with a passage of Scripture or suggestion when there is a pause in the meeting.

Participation.—Encourage ready testimony and prayer, to avoid filling long pauses with songs.
    Call for sentence prayers, if others are not voluntarily offered.
    Confine your opening remarks to from five to ten minutes. Sufficient suggestions can be given in that time for any prayer meeting.
    If possible, ward off "time=killers" and "automatic talkers."
    Take the last five minutes of the meeting for summing up or leaving some thoughts for further study.

Progress.—Seek for originality and advancement in thought or suggestions. It will be a benefit to you and to the meeting.
    Do not try to imitate the leadership of another. Have your own distinctive ideas, keeping in mind the position you occupy and its importance.
    Avoid repetition of incidents or remarks of other leaders, unless specially timely and appropriate.

In arranging for leaders for the prayer meetings, care should be taken to give sufficient time for preparation. Notice should be given at least two weeks in advance of the meeting, unless in exceptional cases.

How long should the leader speak in opening up the topic of the meeting for discussion? Should the leader be limited as to time in his remarks? In a great many cases no restrictions are necessary, as a leader possessing ability and tact will have no difficulty in finding a "period" at the proper time, but unfortunately, there are a great many others who have good intentions, and ability as well, who forget themselves and their auditors, and overreach the time. They have put in a liberal preparation on the subject, until they have seemingly exhausted all the "subject matter," and when the time has come to unfold it, they have conscientiously furnished the meeting with the very last thought that has come to them on the subject, regardless of time consumed or its effect on the meeting. And so, for their benefit, a kindly word of advice is necessary.

Presuming that the ordinary prayer meeting is from one hour to an hour and a quarter in duration, the leader can throw out sufficient suggestions in from five to ten minutes to engage the attention of the meeting for the remainder of the evening. The leader should never occupy longer time than fifteen minutes, even in the most exceptional cases. There are some things that we should expect from our leaders, which, briefly enumerated, are as follows:

1st. Promptness in attendance.
2nd. Promptness in commencing meeting.
3rd. Adherence to the topic of the meeting.
4th. Suggestions on the subject conducive to an interesting meeting.
5th. Brevity of remarks.

6th. Tact in controlling course of meeting.
7th. Recognition of the spiritual side of the meeting.
8th. Promptness in closing the meeting.

It may be well to consider, at this point, the leader's participation or remarks. A paper or "essay" on the topic will no doubt be better than to throw the subject open to the meeting without having said anything about it. A running comment on the different verses in the reading lesson may also be good, but either of these methods are not very apt to encourage or maintain the interest of the prayer meetings.

We expect from the leader some touches of individuality, and at least some evidences of preparation before assuming charge. We also expect that the matter presented will be practical,—nothing of the stereotyped character so often perpetrated in church gatherings; no useless repetition of cant phrases, but matter of vital importance, having to do with the present times, and applicable to all.

In addition to opening up the subject for discussion, it is also a good plan for the leader to take the last two or three minutes, not to exceed five, in summing up what has been said, or in making some special application growing out of the testimonies given.

It occasionally happens that unforseen circumstances will arise preventing the appointed leader from being present. In such an event, the meeting should not be allowed to drag on that account. Have another leader appointed as soon as notice is received, and if the time is too short to give preparation for the topic, have the meeting turned into a praise or consecration service. The meeting should not suffer, whatever course is pursued. In a great many instances, if notice is given prior to the evening of the meeting, the substitute has opportunity to confer with the appointed leader and obtain some of the points or ideas that were to have been used, and in this way will be enabled to do better justice by the meeting, while the people are likely to be better served than they would be by an eleventh-hour preparation.

Notwithstanding all the precautions taken by the Devotional Committee or by those in charge of this service, the leader, nothing daunted, may happen to overrun his time, so that but few minutes are left for the members; the topic has been nearly exhausted, and no one desires to say anything. What are you going to do about it? Should the matter be passed by without comment and the brother or sister thanked for his or her kindly services and congratulated on the good meeting? There are multitudes of Christian people who would do this very thing and yet at the same time feel dreadfully bored by the whole meeting. Why not come out plainly and tell them what is thought about it? Do it in a proper Christian spirit. Say that they took up too much time; and if anything was said not in accord with good doctrine, mention that also; and the leader will in most cases appreciate the kindly suggestions.

If, however, it is necessary to use the same leader again and the same course is again adopted, regardless of the suggestions made, call attention once more to the matter and then let the offender severely alone for a time.

In smaller societies, where material for leaders is scarce, a rotation of leaders is possibly more advantageous than a continued leadership under the same person, unless the latter is especially gifted and is exerting large influence.

In addition to the change of leaders suggested, it will no doubt be helpful to obtain leaders from other churches, and often to better advantage, if of like faith and church membership. New ideas and new life infused may be the means of giving a new impetus to future meetings in the local church leadership.

If topic cards are prepared or prayer meetings arranged without them, for a period covering from one to three or six months, and it is desired to have the meetings specially directed along a particular line, as, for instance, on Bible Knowledge, Prayer, Church Work, Conversion, etc., no better method can be devised than by having the chairman of the committee, or the pastor, if possible, call the leaders together and lay before them the special lines that should be followed, having the matter thoroughly understood and prayed over.

Considerable stress has been laid on the leader, since observation tends to show that a leader such as we have outlined as desirable, will in most cases conduct a prayer meeting successfully, and this is what each church greatly needs if it would prosper in spiritual things.

XIV.
SUBJECT MATTER FOR PRAYER MEETINGS.

So many lines of thought suggest themselves to a Bible student as helpful for the consideration of individuals or societies, that a committee is almost at a loss to know which to use first or to decide which will be most helpful. At the present time, the selection of topics for the young people's meetings, Christian Endeavor, B. Y. P. U., etc., is being done by the National Organization, so that much of this work is not now necessary. The system of having uniform prayer meeting topics in different churches at the same time, has many helpful features:

1. Those who are away from home and attending another prayer meeting, are prepared wherever they go.
2. Difficulty or uncertainty as to topics for consideration is avoided.
3. Unity of study and prayer is helped.

In addition to the young people's meetings, the regular church prayer meeting, an enquirers' meeting, other meetings are usually held from time to time, and for these some suggestions may be fitting.

There are four different classes or styles of subjects that may be followed:

1. Topical and Bible Readings, as for instance on:
   Faith.
   Temperance.
   Holiness.
   Salvation, etc.
2. Devotional:
   The Lord's presence with His people.
   The Power of Prayer.
   One's Duty to Christ.
3. Biographical:
   Moses.
   David.
   Saul.
4. Historical:
   Lesson from God's dealings with Israelites.
   God's plans given by His prophets.
   The early Christian Church our Example.
5. Illustrated:
   The Prodigal Son.
   Wise and Unwise Foundations.
   Giving to Christ or Wasting.

If topics are picked at random throughout the Bible, while some little advantage may be gained in taking a surface glance over the Book, yet the knowledge acquired is about as helpful to the individual as a similar process undergone by a student at school in any of the elementary branches of education—which in fact is nothing but a surface knowledge. For this reason a set course or line of study is specially helpful. The B. Y. P. U. have for some time past selected the prayer meeting topics from the daily Bible readings followed in their C. C. Courses. Those who follow the daily reading are thus better fitted to take part in the prayer meeting than in the old way.

Another method for giving variation to the subjects discussed in the meetings is to have the different committees or organizations represented in the church take charge of the meeting for one or two nights, developing the thoughts nearest to their work; one committee being followed by another throughout the church. This will enable the church to know the spiritual power represented by the different societies or departments.

Again, there are different conditions existing in the church at different times in the year. At one time there seems to be a lack of interest in church work; at another there is an abundance of workers but seeming lack of spiritual power; then the time comes for special meetings and not only workers are needed but earnest prayerful Christians. In order to meet these different conditions the conduct of the prayer meeting can well be directed in keeping therewith and doubtless to good advantage.

Still another and helpful way to make the prayer meetings not only interesting but instructive, is to take a book of the Bible and study it carefully, by chapter or sections, selecting some principal thought in the chapter or section, and making this the pivotal thought. Thus continue until the book has been thoroughly discussed and understood, and so on through the other books of the Bible.

At least one evening in the month should be devoted to the cause of missions. Plan to make this meeting interesting, bright and helpful. Have letters written to missionaries at different mission stations and read their replies at the meetings.

Occasionally it will be well to vary the usual order of exercises and have instead of the regular routine, a special programme prepared. Have one or two solos or quartettes (gospel hymns or religious songs), an instrumental number, an essay on some interesting religious character or subject, or a dialogue. Make the meeting spiritual in its tone throughout, and it will help to renew interest in prayer meeting gatherings.

XV.
PRAYER MEETING MUSIC.

In order that the prayer meeting may be most helpful and interesting, the conducting of the music will have a great deal to do with it. There should be a disposition cultivated amongst the members for earnest "soulful" singing. Ask the members to come prepared with one or two hymns to be sung, suggesting them at the proper time, so that there may be no delay at the meetings. If but few are able to sing correctly, encourage the disposition to sing, even if there is not the ability. How many young people are able to sing in company or for an evening's entertainment outside the church, who profess inability when it comes to helping in their own church. If the writer, by calling attention to this grievous mistake on the part of many of our young ladies and gentlemen, can remedy this difficulty, he will feel that he has done some little good

The chorister or leader should be something more than a combination of a music stand and a windmill. He should sing heartily, cheerfully, and with expression, as if in sympathy with his singing. In order to do this, he or she should be an earnest Christian. There will then be a responsive feeling on the part of those who engage in the singing.

In order that the singing may be vigorous and uplifting, the songs selected should be such as are familiar. At intervals it is well to learn a few new pieces, for too frequent repetitions are apt to be hurtful.

The service of song should be made a feature of worship and not used only for filling in time when the meeting drags. If we bear in mind, in our service of songs, to whom and of whom we sing, and seek to make this a helpful feature, we will accomplish much.

Let the songs selected be such as will give inspiration, spirituality, and enthusiasm. There should be nothing of the interludes or lullaby kind. It is often the case that when there is a long pause and no one offers to take part or to respond at the leader's request, that a song is resorted to. The singing of a song as a means of tiding over the neglect of members to participate, is not always wise. Those who take part in the singing and those who do not know full well the motive that prompts the song. The purpose of the prayer meeting should be spiritual uplifting in prayer and praise to God for His dealings and for their continuance. If we sing for the sake of avoiding an embarassing period of silence "My Jesus I love thee," "Consecrate me now," "More Holiness give me," etc., and the singing does not come from the heart but is only the expression of our lips, ostensibly to kill time, are we not insincere, and may we not be a stumbling-block to the unconverted who construe our every act of service as not being from the heart and willing service. Let a pause occasionally be used for silent prayer and meditation, after which have two or three earnest prayers for the Master's presence to revive, build up, and renew His people in their Christian work, in their example to others, and in their acknowledgement of and confession to Him in the meetings. This will be a change from continually resorting to singing, and no doubt will be more helpful.

If in the introduction of new hymn books, or if the songs selected from the one in use do not seem to call forth sufficient volume of song, it will be wise to have the leader arrange to remain fifteen or twenty minutes after service to drill the members on some of the new hymns best adapted for use. If it cannot be done in this way, probably it can be arranged to have the practice before the meeting.

To add variety to the musical features of the meeting, an occasional solo or quartette of a gospel hymn or strictly religious song, will no doubt be a valuable adjunct; or the introduction of a cornet, violin or harp, might be wise at rare intervals. These features may be combined, and a special musical programme in connection with a topic such as "Praise to God," "Ways in which we can show our praise and thanksgiving," will be very beneficial.

Changes of the character intimated should not be given with a view of seeking something to please the fancy, or to find something to take the place of prayer meetings, or for any other reason than the desire to make the prayer meeting helpful, attractive and interesting.

XVI.
PARTICIPATION BY MEMBERS.

While a great deal depends on the leader of the prayer meeting, the manner in which he deals with the topic, and the time left available for testimony, still the success of the meeting largely depends on how the members assist. One thing more than any other that has had a tendency to injure prayer gatherings, has been the constant repetition on the part of a few of their early conversion, dating twenty, thirty or forty years back. This to them has been the only thing that has made a religious impression on them, and so they cling to it and seek constantly to impress others with it, until it becomes so old and threadbare that we often wish they would go and do something that would give them a new experience. Don't continue to relate second-hand or old-time experiences in the prayer meetings. As you pray each day for your daily bread, so also pray for new experiences, and new views of God's Word and Work, and use them when received.

There are but few members who take part in

the meetings who are as gladly and eagerly listened to as those who are prepared. He who would have the best preparation will keep the meeting in mind during the week, select some thought from the reading lesson from which the topic is chosen, take the one verse that impresses him most and endeavor to have some timely thought or suggestion in connection with it when the evening of the meeting arrives. If no announcement has been made of either topic or reading lesson, some verse of Scripture that has fastened itself upon the mind from daily devotional reading may be considered in its connection with our daily life and made the subject of a brief, purposeful talk. Perchance in reading, a chain of Bible verses has been found and their presentation may be helpful. An application of some new thought in connection with a Bible illustration or Bible character, giving a new idea of some feature of Christian life, may not be amiss.

In addition to matter suggested in connection with God's word, our daily experiences may sometimes suggest new difficulties contended with, battles in which we were defeated or triumphant, or something that has given us new cause for trust in Christ. Such testimonies are always refreshing and serviceable.

If in our perusal of the daily papers, current magazines, or religious periodicals, our attention is drawn to other Christian lives and experiences, to the views or position of others towards the church, and where such matter has no tendency to encourage argument or departure from the line of thought of the meeting, it may be quoted or referred to; and will likely be listened to eagerly. Preparation along any one of the above lines will always be a source of help and encouragement to the prayer meeting

In prayer meeting testimonies or prayers the speaker should always be natural. He should not seek to imitate the voice and manner of older and wiser persons or to adopt language or terms employed by them. Be original but be modest, be what you are or at least what you seem to be to others, and you will be better appreciated.

It is always best to take part promptly and voluntarily; you are then very apt to know what you want to say and more likely to say it in a satisfactory manner. If called upon to speak or pray without warning, many persons are likely to do themselves an injustice.

A great deal is said of the value of personal experience in testimony, and there is no doubt that to many it carries much weight; but while following this line, do not forget that God's Word is a storehouse of information, and from its pages much of help,—promises, others' experiences, others' difficulties and triumphs, are recounted—is certain to be an aid to every one. Remember how the Psalmist David prized the Word and follow his example. If you do this it will always prompt you, so that you will be ready to give an answer to any that ask you regarding the hope within you.

What shall we say of those who have no voice or part in the meeting? Remember the Master's Words—"Whosoever shall deny me before men, him will I also deny before my father in heaven," and again —" If any man will be my disciple, let him deny himself and take up his cross and follow me."

Let us consider this matter thoughtfully as friend with friend. When we went to school and were associated with other scholars in the same room, were we too timid to recite or answer questions of the teacher in the class? Did we remain silent and lose the benefit we would have gained by our recitation? As we grew older and mingled with society and when the room was filled with other young people enjoying the same games, were we afraid to take a prominent part in the game when called upon because we were too timid, and did we remain silent? Then when we got still older and entered into business relations in offices where large numbers were employed, and we were singled out before all the others to do some important errand, or answer some question regarding our work, were we silent?

Now, on the other hand, realizing what Jesus has done for us, and the love that has led Him to save us, should we allow opportunity to go by unheeded without confessing Him or saying even the feeblest word for him? My friend, if you have heretofore been silent, pray God to help you to speak for Him and then speak—He will surely help you. Members can help those who are timid by speaking a kindly word to them in the meeting after they have taken part, or commending them when they themselves are taking part. Above all, criticism should be avoided as it will do more to drive them from testifying again than anything else. If a new member rises and stammers and stutters, yet says a few words feelingly and sits down, give him a hearty hand-shake and a word of encouragement, but do not criticise or speak lightly of his effort. One method by which a testimony or statement of some kind may be obtained, is by roll call. Announce that it will be by verse,—a promise, a favorite passage, etc.,—and the timid or indifferent will be helped to say something, however brief. In unavoidable absence from the meeting, a letter expressing your love for Christ or desire to do His service, will not be out of place.

To a large majority of young people, it does

not seem so difficult a matter to give a few words of testimony, but to engage in public prayer seems beyond their ability. One reason for this undoubtedly is that we have been educated to expect that a public prayer is not complete without it deals with different branches of church work, home and foreign missions, national and city affairs, the denomination, members wherever scattered, etc., etc., so that when a venerable deacon or other officer of the church offers an earnest prayer embracing all these different features, young people are afraid to venture their feeble petition, fearing criticism or that it is not as worthy. Don't believe it, my friend. The prayer of the poor publican was very brief and possibly was uttered with much misgiving, but it expressed his heartfelt want: "Lord be merciful to me a sinner," and the record reads that he went down to his house justified.

The leader should encourage sentence prayers or testimonies. This will soon give confidence to add other petitions specially desired, and the feeling of timidity or uncertainty will soon vanish.

A brief but earnest prayer out of the heart of a sincere Christian is far more beneficial in its influence than many of what has been termed by a leading clergymen "pyrotechnic displays." Possibly it may be helpful to the members for the pastor or leader to ask for requests for prayers; thus in stating what special burden is upon his heart, a member may be led also to take part in prayer in the meeting. It would also be well to encourage among members, who do not expect to be present at the prayer meeting, written requests for prayer if they have anything that they feel is worthy of this attention and consideration. Among some denominations the prayer meeting partakes largely of the character of an experience meeting. A great many false conceptions are prevalent as to what forms the basis of a religious experience. My own pastor, Dr. Lawrence, gives three fundamental characteristics as the basis:

1—God's Word studied and obeyed.
2—Loyalty to Christ.
3—Readiness to suffer.

If the experiences through which we pass from time to time come under any one of these three topics, we have something to tell that will be helpful to the prayer meeting.

One other feature that we should also cultivate, is growth and development in our participation in the meetings. If we do this, we shall need to make progress in Bible knowledge, in Christian growth, in usefulness in religious work, and above all, in the power of winning souls to Christ. The last feature transcends all others and should be considered paramount.

XVII.
A MODEL PRAYER MEETING.

With all the changes that the centuries have wrought in human progress and thought, it scarcely seems possible that we can look back to the foundation of the early church, and find in their first gatherings for prayer the elements that largely constitute a Model Prayer Meeting. We read that "They continued steadfastly in the apostle's doctrine and fellowship, in breaking of bread and in prayers," and "they continued daily with one accord in the temple praising God and having favor with all the people, resulting in the fact that "the Lord added to the church daily such as should be saved."

Here are some suggestions that we can profit by in the conduct of our prayer meetings. The model prayer meeting will not have stereotyped or formal addresses; the testimonies that are given, the prayers offered, or the songs sung, will be from the heart, voluntary, able and effective. The meeting will be of such a character as to interest young and old alike, and both may look forward to it with pleasure. It will not partake of the nature of a debating society as to formal or strict observance of rules, but will be conducted in an orderly, prompt, and deliberate manner. Neither will the participation be of the style indicated, but all things will be done in keeping with the service.

The model prayer meeting will be conducted in such a manner that, after the meeting is over, the members will not feel wearied by the length or character of the service.

A meeting of this kind will be one that will bring the members in closer touch with the Master, give them a great spiritual uplifting, and revive and refresh them for their daily duties and burdens. The meeting will also be one where frequent testimonies are made regarding work done, personal experiences related, conversions expected or already effected, or anything of this nature that may be deemed helpful.

One thing that will always be sought for by the leader will be to keep the meeting out of ruts—out of moving along in a lifeless, mechanical manner, so that it will require power, life and energy combined to make it a success.

The model prayer meeting has its every feature conducted with life and energy The leader, choristers and members each fill their place promptly and without hesitation. The prayers offered, the songs sung, and the testimonies given are all rendered with promptness and with vigor.

The topic has been announced, so that all have had an opportunity for preparation for the meeting. The speaker's talks are practical and helpful, and this idea is kept in mind in making preparation for the meeting.

The participants in prayer meetings of this kind are not confined to any one class, but young, middle aged, and old people alike have opportunity to take part in the meeting.

As the members assemble before the hour set for the prayer meeting and as they retire at the close, there will be sociability shown amongst the people—a hearty hand-shake or a kindly greeting, wherever possible. No unkind remarks will be made of other members. Outside gossip or scandal will have no place. Those who take part, whether in testimony or prayer, will show indications of growth, not only in freedom and confidence in taking part, but also in the religious knowledge that they have acquired.

The model prayer meeting will be attended by those who observe the five "P's":

Prayer for the Meeting.
Presence in the Meeting.
Preparation for the Meeting.
"Period" in taking part.
Purpose after the Meeting.

XVIII.
COMMITTEE WORK AT PRAYER MEETINGS.

The half hour following the prayer meeting affords an excellent opportunity for planning religious work for the different associations or organizations of the church. At this time leaders, workers, contributions, and helps of various kinds may be secured. Here is a good opportunity to enquire or look after absentees or get new scholars for the Sunday-school, to secure teachers for classes, and to get visitors to look up those who have been irregular in their attendance or have dropped out. The opportunity is also presented to obtain leaders for the prayer meetings, to speak to those unaccustomed to take part, and get them to promise to read a verse or take some part at the next meeting, or for asking members to attend to other features pertaining to the meetings.

Now also is the best opportunity for making acquaintance with the members and for meeting those who are strangers or are not well-known. It can also be arranged at this time to have some of the young men introduced into different homes to spend an evening, and thus wield an influence over them during the week. Social gatherings may also be planned, but as many as possible of the minor details should be left until another time, that the desired results of the prayer meeting may not be effaced.

Opportunity may also be taken to secure more members for the young people's societies or to inquire regarding those absent. Officers or chairmen for the different committees may also be selected or engaged, and invitations extended to members to attend certain of the meetings, where they can be of assistance.

Tracts, temperance or devotional literature, or other matter of religious import may here be distributed to good advantage.

Subscriptions, contributions, or other funds for different branches of church work outside of the regular church subscriptions or dues, can be arranged or adjusted at this time.

Objection may be raised by some to the use of the time before and after the prayer meeting for the purposes mentioned, but if each matter is gone about judiciously, much of the negotiations and arrangements that are now made on Sunday, will be adjusted on a week day, which will commend itself to every thoughtful person desiring freedom to worship God and to receive such benefits as come from the Sunday services.

XXI.
TOPICS AND ANALYSES.

Individual Responsibility.—John 21: 20-24.
(a) The gospel call is to individuals.
(b) Christ selected individuals for his work.
(c) The Church founded on individual efforts.
(d) See that we are right before criticising others—
Judge not that ye be not judged.
(e) We are judged individually.
Note Christ's remark to Peter: "What is that to thee; follow thou me."

Effectual Prayer.—Jas. 5: 15-18.
(a) There should be a purpose in prayer.
(b) Petitions should be earnest and direct.
(c) Faith should be shown to expect an answer.
(d) Prayer should be urgent and repeated.
Note Abraham pleading for Sodom; Elijah and the prophets of Baal.

Evidences of Conversion.—2 Cor. 5: 17; Rom. 8: 9.
(a) New desires
(b) A new life and a changed life.
(c) Desire to acknowledge Christ.
(d) Desire to work for Christ.
(e) Showing the spirit of Christ.
Note Paul's conversion. The conversion of Lydia.

A Discouraged Christian.—1 Kings 19: 1-18.
(a) First steps in discouragement.
(b) Occasions for discouragement.
(c) How discouragements may be avoided.
(d) Antidote.
Note God's Word to Elijah, to Jonah, to Moses.

What can we say for Christ.—Acts 4: 13-21.
- (a) What has Christ done for you.
- (b) What reasons have we for testimony.
- (c) Some elements of testimony.
- (d) Our claims on Christ.

Note: Early disciples.—Early martyrs.

Christian Stability.—Col. 2: 6-7.
- (a) Stability essential in material and worldly things.
- (b) Dangers surrounding an unstable man.
- (c) Where stability should be expected.
- (d) How stability may be attained.
- (e) Illustrations—Joseph, Samuel, Paul, Stephen, etc.

The above outline analysis may be suggestive to leaders in dealing with other topics of which a selection is hereafter given. The leader should aim to have at least from five to six different suggestive ideas regarding the topic which can be developed by the members present. Suggestions and ideas should be brief and pointed, and sufficient only to lead up to the thoughts and so give the members something to talk upon that may be interesting to the meeting.

TOPICS WITH TEXTS.

The Christian.
- Christian Character in responsible places. 2 Chron. 19: 1-11.
- Christian rejoicing. 1 Peter 4: 12-19.
- Christian conversation. 1 Peter 3: 8-16.
- Christian example. Rom. 12: 9-21.
- Christian influence. Mark 6: 20.
- Christian conflict. 2 Tim. 3: 1-15.
- Christian armor and its use. Eph. 6: 10-18.
- Christian courage. 2 Chr. 32: 1-8.

Christian trial. 1 Peter 4: 12-19.
Christian in business. Neh. 5: 1-13.
Christian watchfulness. Matt. 25: 1-13.
Christian light. Matt. 5: 14-16.
Christian hope. 1 Thes. 2: 19; 1 Cor. 2: 9.
Christian joy. John 15: 11.

GENERAL TOPICS.

Certainties:
  Forgiveness of sins.
  God's promises.
  God's judgments.
  Saved or unsaved.

The Christian:
  The Christian at Home.
  The Christian in Business.
  The Christian in Society.
  What is a Christian?
  What the Christian can do.
  What the Christian may be.

Reading God's Word.
  (a) How.
  (b) When.
  (c) Where.

Studying and memorizing God's Word.
  Application of God's Word to enquirers.
  Application of God's Word to personal life.

Duty or Example:
  Christ our example.
  What the Savior has done for us.
  Our duty to Christ.
  Our example.

Christian Work.
  (a) The work.
  (b) The worker.
  (c) Preparation for work.
  (d) Power to work.
  (e) Motives for work.
  (f) Qualification for work.
  (g) Our responsibility.

Belief or Unbelief.
- (a) Folly of unbelief.
- (b) What the Bible says of the unbelieving.
- (c) Unbelief made saving faith.
- (d) Promises to believers.
- (e) Duties of believers.
- (f) Believers' blessings.

Phases of Christian Life.
Faith, Assurance, Obedience, Justice, Goodness, Suffering, Service, Giving, Prayer, Sincerity, Sacrifice, Zealousness, Patience, Benevolence, Humility, Forgiveness, Affliction, Continuance, Conversation, Worship, Courage, etc., etc.

God's Word.
Inspired. 2 Tim. 3: 16 and 17.
Sufficient. Luke 16: 31.
Its completeness. Ps. 19: 7–11.
Its use. Deut. 6: 6 and 7.
Should be read. John 5: 39.
" " obeyed. 1 Pet. 4: 17.
" " loved. Deut. 6: 4–9.
" " understood. Luke 24: 45.
" " meditated upon. Ps. 1: 2.
" " lived up to. Josh. 1: 8.
Helps to conversion. Acts 8: 35–37.
" " the soul's cleansing. Eph. 5: 26.
" " spiritual growth. 1 Pet. 2: 2.
It warns of evil. Ps. 119: 9–11.
It exposes sin. Rom. 3: 22–25.
It tells of heaven. John 14: 6.
It lights our way. Ps. 119: 105.
His teachings to guide us.
His example to stimulate us.
His promises to help us.

MISCELLANEOUS TOPICS.

The security of the Godly. Ps. 91: 1–16.
Hearing and doing. Jas. 1: 22–27.
A gift for all. John 3: 16.
A wise resolution. Phil. 3: 13–16.
Precepts for daily living. Josh. 1: 7–9.

Some things to think about. Phil. 4: 8.
Resisting evil. Heb. 12: 1-6.
With or without God, Which? Eph. 2: 12 and 13.
Excuses. Luke 14: 16-24.
Worldly faith or faith in God. Ps. 49: 6-20.
Opportunity for work. Joel 3: 13 and 14.
Pure religion. Jas. 1: 26 and 27.
Our equipment. 2 Tim. 3: 14-17.
Blessings of serving God. Prov. 3: 1-6.
What have I received from Christ. Ps. 103: 2.
God's Word defeats evil purposes. 2 Chr. 11: 1-5.
Answered prayers. 2 Kings 19: 14-20; 32-36.
What we have by believing in Christ. 1 Pet. 1: 3-9.
Almost persuaded. Acts 24: 24-26; Acts 26: 24-29.
Fully persuaded. Acts 8: 27-39.
Testifying amidst unbelievers. Luke 22: 54-62.
Disowning Christ. Luke 22: 54-62.
Half-hearted service. 2 Chron. 25: 2.
Temptations and how to avoid them. Matt. 4: 1-11.
The reward of obedience. Deut. 28: 1-14.
True possessions and how to gain them. Luke 12:13-34.
Whole-hearted service. Eph. 6: 5-18
God's care for our daily needs. Matt. 6: 25-33.
A discouraged man satisfied. John 5: 1-14.
One who feared God rather than man. Dan. 6: 4-11; 25-28.
Returning to God. 2 Chr. 30: 1-9.
Rest in Christ. Matt. 11: 28.
Thanksgiving. Psalm 68: 19.
Some things we know. 1 John 5: 10-15.
God's Word read and understood. Neh. 8: 1-8.
Justified freely. Rom. 3: 24-26.
Weak excuses for failing to testify. Ex. 4: 10-12.
God's presence with His people. Ex. 40: 34-38.
Benefits of Sabbath observance. Lev. 26: 2-12.
Precepts for Christian workers. Josh. 1: 7-9.
Wholly following the Lord. Josh. 14: 5-14.
God's call, our reponse. 1 Sam. 3: 3-10.
Whom God rejects. 1 Sam. 15: 18-24.
God's standard of judgment. 1 Sam. 16: 1-8.
Present and future blessings from service. 2 Sam. 7: 8-16.
Conditions upon which blessings are given. 1 Kings 9: 2-9.

Folly of heeding unwise counsel. 1 Kings 12: 8-14.
God provides for our daily needs. " 17: 3-16.
God answers true prayer. " 18: 30-39.
How God reveals Himself. " 19: 11-13.
Our excuses for discouragaments. " 19: 14-18.
Ill-gotten gains useless. " 21: 6-19.
Obedience brings its reward. 2 Kings 5: 6-16.
Deceitfulness punished. " 5: 20-27.
Serving God in high places. " 18: 1-7.
How we may know God. 2 Chr. 33: 12-13.
Burden bearing. Gal. 6. 1-6.
The Christ walk. Eph. 4: 1-6; 17-32.
Right and wrong ways of seeking. Ecc. 1: 12-18.
True growth. Eph. 4: 11-16.
Looking backward. Ps. 145: 1-21.
Different ways of rejecting Christ. Mark 15: 6-14.
Bringing others to Christ. 1 Cor. 9: 19-27.
Systematic giving. Mal. 3: 7-12.
Self-control. Col. 3: 1-15.
Keeping the Sabbath Day. Mark 2: 23-28.
God's promises and their proofs. Heb. 6: 9-20.
Cross bearing. Matt. 10: 37-39.
Lifting up Christ. John 3: 14-15.
The Christian's life in the world. Eph. 4: 20-32.
How we may preach Christ. 2 Tim. 4: 1-10.
Sowing the seed. Isa. 32: 20.
Our Father's House. John 14: 2-16.
Fruit bearing. John 15: 2.
Lesson from Judas. Matt. 26: 14-16.
Afraid to do right. Luke 23: 23-24.
Secret prayer. Mark 1: 35.
Not far from the kingdom. Mark 12: 34.
How we can show that we are God's children. John 8: 31; 15: 1-8.
Are we also blind. John 9: 40 and 41.
He died that we might live. 2 Cor. 5: 14-15. 1 John 3: 16.
How men are helped by the Holy Spirit. John 16: 7-14.
Christ's lowliness our example. Isa. 53: 1-12.
On which side am I? Josh. 24: 14-16.
Victory. Romans 8: 31-39.
Stand fast. Gal. 5: 1.
Blest to bless. Matt. 10: 7-8; 38: 42.
Wordliness in the church. John 2: 13-17.

The Alternatives. John 3: 16-21; 31 and 36.
Stumbling Blocks. 1 Cor. 8-13.
Christian meditation. Ps. 1: 2.
Practical Godliness. Gal. 5: 14.
Our commission. Acts 22: 15.
Profit and Loss. Mark 8: 34-37.
The disciple whom Jesus loved. John 13: 23.
Lovest thou me. John 21: 15-17.
Our recognition of the Gospel. Rom. 1; 16.
What shall the harvest be. Gal. 6: 7.
Looking forward. Phill. 3: 13 and 14.
Motives for service. Col. 3: 23 and 24.
Something every Christian can do. 1 Thes. 5: 14-15.
Our young people's example. 1 Tim. 4: 12 and 13.
Some things that are hurtful. Titus 3: 9.
Martyrs for Christ. Heb. 11: 37 and 38.
The Efficacy of Prayer. Jas. 5: 13-18.
Chosen for what. 1 Pet. 2: 9.
The Christian's arithmetic. 2 Pet. 1; 5-7. Acts. 9: 31. 2 Tim. 2: 15. John 1: 29.
Conditions to receiving answered prayers. 1 John 3: 22.
Hindrances to the Church. 3 John 9 and 10.
Four essentials of Christian life. Jude 20 and 21.
A solemn occasion. Rev. 20: 11-15.
A searching question. Gen. 3; 8 and 9.
God's knowledge of us. Gen. 18: 17-19.
Our Covenant with God. Gen. 28: 20-22.
Results of our indifference. Prov. 1: 24-28.
Contrasts between evil and good. Prov. 2: 21 and 22.
Acknowledgement of God brings guidance. Prov. 3: 6.
The two paths. Prov. 4: 14-19.
Small objects teach great lessons. Prov. 6: 6-11.
Some things the Lord despises. Prov. 6: 16-19.
Heeding parental counsels. Prov. 6: 20-23.
Nearness to God, how known. Prov. 15: 29.
The value of a good name. Prov. 22: 1.
Effects of intemperance. Prov. 23: 29-32.
Wise treatment of enemies. Prov. 25: 21 and 22.
What shall we do with our sins. Prov. 28: 13.
Lessons from little things. Prov. 30: 24-28.
Christian work profitable. Prov. 12: 30 and 31.
Benefits of wisdom. Prov. 4: 5-9.
Exemplary Christian life. Ps. 1: 1-2.
Ungodliness disastrous. Ps. 1: 4-6.

God's view of those who disregard Him. Ps. 1: 2-5.
The first element of mission work. Ps. 2: 8.
True recognition of God's goodness. Ps. 4: 1 and 2.
A true Christian citizen. Ps. 15: 1-5.
God's judgment on the wicked. Ps. 9: 17.
God's place with His people. Ps. 16: 8 and 9.
The Christian's attitude to God. Ps. 18: 2.
Some things that are right. Ps. 19: 7-9.
Prayer for right thoughts and speech. Ps. 19 : 14.
The Christian's trust in God. Ps. 23: 1-4.
Unswerving confidence in God. Ps. 27: 1-5.
Blessings of confessing our sins. Ps. 32: 1-5.
One way to avoid evil speaking. Ps. 34: 1.
Some things to avoid doing. Ps. 34: 13 and 14.
God's power shown. Ps. 33: 6-11.
Consecrated speech. Ps. 35: 28.
Christian character shown in daily life. Ps. 37: 3-7.
Helpful Christian silence. Ps. 39: 1-3.
Confidence in God. Ps. 40: 1-3.
God's care of the Poor. Ps. 41: 1-3.
Implicit confidence in God. Ps. 46: 1-7.
An earnest prayer for forgiveness and restoration. Ps. 51: 1-13.
Daily private prayer. Ps. 55: 17.
Where our burdens may be left. Ps. 55: 22.
God's blessings bestowed upon all. Ps. 65: 9-13.
Voluntary testimony. Ps. 66: 13-20.
God's patience with His children. Ps. 78: 35-38.
The Christian's desire for church services. Ps. 84: 1-10
Blessedness of serving God. Ps. 84: 11 and 12.
Brevity of human life. Ps. 90: 9-12.
God's protection to His people. Ps. 91: 1-16.
The prosperity of the righteous. Ps. 92: 12-14.
Proper recognition of God. Ps. 96: 1-10.
God's greatness and power. Ps. 97: 1-6.
Cheerful worship. Ps. 100: 1-5.
A covenant with God. Ps. 101: 1-8.
A discouraged Christian. Ps: 102: 1-12.
Hope for the discouraged. Ps. 102: 16-28.
How God forgives sins. Ps. 103: 3-13.
God's Great Providences. Ps. 104: 1-24.
Constant praise to God. Ps. 104: 33 and 34.
God's leniency with those who forget Him. Ps. 106: 7-15.
How to overcome enemies. Ps. 109: 2-4.

Present promises to the Godly. Ps. 112: 1-3.
Christian possessions. Ps. 112: 7 and 8.
What we expect of the Church. Ps. 112: 9.
Worldly view of the Christian. Ps. 112: 10.
Vanity of worshiping anything else in place of God. Ps. 115: 2-9.
The Lord our support and shield. Ps. 118: 6-16.
Happiness in serving God. Ps. 119: 1-7.
God's word a daily guide. Ps. 119: 9-11.
A prayer for enlightenment. Ps. 119: 18 and 27.
Some suggestions as to our testimony. Ps. 119: 28-31.
Good companions—How obtained. Ps. 119: 63.
Delight in God's Word. Ps. 119: 89-112.
An earnest prayer for guidance. Ps. 119: 133-135.
God's protection to His saints. Ps. 121: 1-8.
Our love for God's House. Ps. 122: 1-9.
Safety in trusting God. Ps. 125: 1 and 2.
Comfort for Christian workers. Ps. 126: 6.
Temporal blessings in serving God. Ps. 128: 1-6.
Christian unity desirable. Ps. 133: 1-3.
Serving God outside the church. Ps. 137: 4.
No escape from God. Ps. 139: 7-12.
God searching for evil. Ps. 139: 23 and 24.
Helplessness without God. Ps. 142: 4.
When God answers prayer. Ps. 145: 18 and 19.
A reason for praising God. Ps. 147: 1.
Abiding with Christ. John 1:39.
The true spirit of discipleship. John 1: 41 and 42.
Our use of God's House. John 2: 14-16.
The gospel demands plainly stated. John 3: 36.
Why Christ is rejected. John 5: 40.
Our reasons for following Christ. John 6: 26 and 27.
Loyalty to Christ. John 6: 66 and 67.
What constitutes a true disciple. John 8: 31 and 32.
Our knowledge of conversion. John 9: 25.
The certainty of our salvation. John 10: 27 and 28.
Ambassadors for Christ. John 13: 20.
Prepared mansions. John 14: 1-4.
Personal contact with Christ necessary. John 15: 1-7.
Has our work obtained results. John 15: 16.
The Christian's mission in the world. John 17: 15-17.
An unbeliever convinced. John 20: 28.
How to obtain helpers in church work. John 21: 3.
Proofs of Christ's coming. Acts 1: 3.

The work and the preparation. Acts 1: 8.
How to choose Christian workers. Acts 1: 22-24.
Gospel work brings results. Acts 2: 42, 46 and 47.
Whom God uses in His work. Acts 4: 13.
Christian convictions in dangerous places. Acts 4: 18-20.
The power of prayer. Acts 4: 31.
Christian something more than in name. Acts 5: 40-42.
Following Christ in suffering. Acts 7: 59 and 60.
An example for Christian womanhood. Acts 9: 36-39.
Needful preparation for successful service. Acts 11: 22-24.
God's Word without limitations. Acts 13: 46.
Rejoicing in tribulations. Acts 16: 22-28.
Certainty of God's support. Acts 18: 9 and 10.
Some good advice for thoughtless Christians. Acts 20: 32.
Effect of God's Word on unbelievers. Acts 24: 24 and 25.
Believing God amidst difficulties. Acts 27: 22-25.
Morality does not give safety. Rom. 3: 23.
How to obtain peace. Rom. 5: 1.
Salvation through Christ. Rom. 5: 6-10.
Our choice of two gifts. Rom. 6: 23.
No class distinctions in the Gospel. Rom. 10: 13.
Reasonable and unreasonable service. Rom. 12: 1.
Self-esteem. Rom. 12: 3.
Our hindrances to other Christians. Rom. 14: 13.
Giving a means of grace. Rom. 15: 26 and 27.
Whom God chooses to work for Him. 1 Cor. 1: 26-28.
Heaven's mysteries inconceivable. 1 Cor. 2: 9.
A sure foundation. 1 Cor. 3: 11 and 12.
Temples intended for service. 1 Cor. 3: 16 and 17.
Tempted by man; fortified by God. 1 Cor. 10: 13.
Evidences of love, how manifested. 1 Cor. 13: 1-7.
The highest principles of the Gospel. 1 Cor. 13: 13.
The Christian's testimony. 1 Cor. 14: 15 and 16.
Advice for Christians. 1 Cor. 15: 58.
Four principles for young Christians. 1 Cor. 16: 13.
How to defeat Satan. 2 Cor. 2: 10-11.
A great charge. 2 Cor. 3: 18.
Some things Christians should avoid. 2 Cor. 4: 2.
The Christian's life not all happiness. 2 Cor. 4: 8-10.
How our Christianity should be made known. 2 Cor. 5: 17.
Our position in Christian work. 2 Cor. 5: 20.

Riches exchanged for poverty. 2 Cor. 8: 9.
The spirit of Christian benevolence. 2 Cor. 9: 7.
Strength shown by weakness. 2 Cor. 12: 10.
Christian rebuke. Gal. 2: 11-17.
Wise use of liberty. Gal. 5: 1 and 3.
A harvest field for all. Gal. 6: 7.
Our first duty in the church. Gal. 6: 10.
How the burden is borne. Gal. 6: 2 and 5.
God's plans for His people. Eph. 1: 9 and 10.
Praying for others. Eph. 1: 15-18.
God's love manifested. Eph. 2: 4-7.
Christian growth—how? Eph. 2: 21 and 22.
What we should preach. Eph. 3: 8 and 9.
The measure of God's gift. Eph. 3: 20.
Oneness of spirit, hope and service. Eph. 4: 3-6.
Our place in God's vineyard. Eph. 4: 11 and 12.
Our expectations of young converts. Eph. 4: 13-15.
A Christian in the world. Eph. 5: 7-13.
Our motive for service. Eph. 6: 6-8.
Prayer for our brothers. Phil. 1: 9-11.
Christian testimony helpful to others. Phil. 1: 14.
True spirit of humility. Phil. 2: 1-3.
Our example to the world. Phil. 2: 14 and 15.
Faithfulness extolled. Phil. 2: 25-30.
Christian contentment. Phil. 4: 11-13.
Five essentials in Christian life. Col. 1: 10-13.
True spirit of forgiveness. Col. 3: 13.
Our place in the prayer meeting. Col. 3: 16 and 17.
Prayer for missionaries. Col. 4: 3.
Christian conduct outside the church. Col. 4: 5 and 6.
Our recognition of work done. 1 Thes. 1: 2 and 3.
The true evangelical spirit. 1 Thes. 2: 1-8.
God's Word rightly received. 1 Thes. 2: 13.
Continuance in prayer. 1 Thes. 3: 10.
The Christian established. 1 Thes. 3: 12 and 13.
Total abstinence. 1 Thes. 5: 22.
Proving and disapproving. 1 Thes. 5: 21.
A church example. 2 Thes. 1: 3 and 4.
God's Word verified. 1 Tim. 3: 16.
Preparation for Christian work. 1 Tim. 4: 13.
Something to fight for. 1 Tim. 6: 12.
Religion in the family. 2 Tim. 1: 5.
Expectations of God's servants. 2 Tim. 2: 24-26.
Purity commended. Titus 1: 15.

Advancement in Christian growth. Heb. 6: 1.
Christ's second coming. Heb. 9: 27 and 28.
Our interest in religious gatherings. Heb. 10: 25.
God's judgment. Heb. 10: 26-31.
Christian's need of patience. Heb. 10: 35-37.
Holiness essential in Christ's kingdom. Heb. 12: 14.
Christian's future. Heb. 12: 22 and 23.
One who never changes. Heb. 13: 8.
A reason for contentment. Heb. 13: 5.
The right use of wealth. 1 Tim. 6: 17-19.
Some things to avoid. 2 Tim. 3: 2 and 3.
Daily living. Titus 2: 11-13.
A fitting example. Heb. 11: 25 and 26.
Pure religion. Jas. 1: 27.
Something worthy of our asking. Jas. 1: 5 and 6.
Worthy and worthless Christians. Jas. 1: 26.
Distinctions in Christ's service. Jas. 2: 1-4.
Manifestations of wisdom. Jas. 3: 17.
Vain boasting. Jas. 4: 13-15.
Four elements of Christian life. Jude 20: 21.
What God can do for us. Jude 24.
Which shall we choose. 1 John 5: 12.
Statements that concern us. 1 John 1: 6-10.
Our calling and preparation for work. 1 Pet. 5: 10.
An enemy to fight. 1 Pet. 5: 8.
Advantages of persecution. 1 Pet. 4: 12-16.
A Christian's attitude to the world. 1 Pet. 2: 13-17.
Distinguishing traits of Christian people. 1 Pet. 2: 9.
Evidences of sin. Jas. 4: 17.
The roll call of the faithful. Heb. 11: 4-39.
A Christian's last words. 2 Tim. 4: 6-8.
Biblical testimony to unbelievers. 1 Tim. 6: 3-5.
The effect of our wrong doing on others. 1 Tim. 5: 24-25.
The source of our gifts. Jas. 1: 17.
Hearing, speaking and doing. Jas. 1: 19.
Vain religion. Jas. 1: 26.
Whom God chooses. Jas. 2: 5.
How to control our speech. Jas. 3: 5-8.
Reasons for unanswered prayers. Jas. 4: 3.
How to come close to God. Jas. 4: 8-10.
The sin of delay. Jas. 4. 17.
Christian worker rewarded. Jas. 5: 20.
Advantage of trials. 1 Pet. 1: 6-7.

Our redemption. 1 Pet. 1: 18 and 19.
A contrast in our condition. 1 Pet. 2: 10.
Our great example. 1 Pet. 2: 21-23.
Mottoes for daily life. 1 Pet. 2: 17.
God's attitude to men. 1 Pet. 3: 12.
Our motive in service. 1 Pet. 5: 2.
A question that concerns us. 2 Pet. 3: 11.
A promise for following Christ. 1 John 1: 7.
Our attitude to the world. 1 John 2: 15.
An unfailing promise. 1 John 2: 25.
The Savior's recognition of thanksgiving. Luke 17: 12-18.
Hindrances to serving Christ. Luke 18: 24 and 25.
Cross-bearing. Luke 23: 26.
What is our witness? Luke 24: 48.
Tarrying for God's spirit. Luke 24: 49.

XIX.
QUESTIONS ANSWERED.

Would you discontinue the prayer meetings in the summer months? Ans. Not while there are the scriptural number of two or three gathered together in the Master's name.

Q. What would you do with those who regularly and profitlessly take up the time of the prayer meeting? Ans. Have one of the most careful and discreet members call on the persons and explain that it injures the prayer meeting and ask them to save some of their surplus matter for another occasion. If this fails, rather than have the prayer meeting killed, have one of the officers insist on briefer remarks or absolute silence.

Q. In announcements of meetings, should the leader's name be given in addition to the subject? Ans. A change of methods is possibly the best plan to adopt. Have your topic cards contain all the names of leaders and subjects; then let the next one only contain the subjects and scripture selections without the leaders. If this plan is followed, there will be no excuse for staying at home on account of knowing the leader, and his or her methods.

Q. How would you encourage the timid or seemingly indifferent to take part in the meetings? Ans. Have two or more members of the lookout or devotional committees speak to the timid or those who have not been taking any part in the meeting, and get them to read a verse of Scripture, a brief paper, or offer a sentence prayer at the next meeting. Make it a point to have these same members again assigned to some part in the meeting in a reasonable period, and by continuing a few times, the timidity or indifference will be worn off and instead a desire to participate in the meetings will be manifested.

Q. How can the prayer meeting service be made auxiliary to the work of the young people? Ans. Each of the committees of the young people's societies should see that some of their number is at the meeting at least half an hour before service and remain after the close of the service. Leaders can then be secured for meetings, and members can be solicited to do various lines of work, etc.

Q. Should a member speak simply for the sake of filling his or her place? Ans. The remembrance of a promise or pledge made may lead to a desire to have an experience or testimony that may be helpful to the meeting, so by simply fulfilling an obligation there may be quickened a desire for voluntary testimony.

Q. If few take part in the meeting, would you close it before time? Ans. When there seems to be no desire for participation in the meeting, the meeting is evidently at a close and it is wiser to adjourn than to kill it or detract from its benefits by long pauses.

Q. How long should a model experience, or one's remarks, be in a prayer meeting? Ans. Sentence testimonies, or those of sufficient length to fully express a single thought.

Q. What should be the length of the prayer meeting? Ans. One hour or one hour and a quarter. Never continue over that limit unless in very exceptional cases, and then for but very few minutes.

Q. If the prayer meeting is not supported or attended by young people, how would you obviate this result? Ans. By personal work, by committee work, by raising the standard of the prayer meetings, and by making them more interesting.

Q. Is it always best for the Devotional Committee to select the subjects instead of the leader? Ans. If you are following a system of uniform topics, yes; but the leader may have the choice of a particular subject if you have sufficient leaders to allow this to be done.

Q. Should young ladies lead prayer meetings? If not, why not? Ans. There exists a division of opinion on this subject. In many churches where the working force is largely composed of young ladies and women, it would seem necessary. In the larger city churches, where there is an abundance of young men, it has not been deemed fitting by some to do so.

Q. What would you do in a society where members take part in the prayer meetings whose conduct after the meetings is not in keeping with their profession at the prayer meeting? Ans. Seek to lead them to a better life, and discourage their testimonies until evidences vouch for it that they are sincere.

Q. What can be done with those who would take part in the prayer meeting but for their extreme timidity? Ans. Urge them to come early, to take seats close to the front, and to take part promptly when the invitation is given. Suggest that they start by reading a Bible verse, then a sentence thought or a sentence prayer, and continue doing so until the fear has lessened and the hesitation has passed away.

Q. If there seems to be an unwillingness in those present to take part in the meeting, is it wise to call on members to speak or lead in prayer? Ans. As an occasional instance, yes; but a continued state of affairs of this kind shows that the members need to be impressed with their responsibility, and with the privilege of growth that the meeting offers. Possibly a personal plea, or a word of encouragement from older and experienced members, may be helpful, and so avoid appealing to this involuntary service.

Q. Would you appoint leaders from week to week? Ans. Only in exceptional cases. Leaders should have from two weeks to two months preparation. Not to prepare an elaborate speech or paper, but to get the best suggestions, the most timely and most helpful thoughts possible, and to have these confined within the briefest compass.

Q. What should be done to interest members in the work who are not good leaders for prayer meetings. Ans. If there are smaller gatherings for prayer than the usual weekly or young people's meeting, let them get experience from these first before attempting larger gatherings. When they lead, let all the members rally round them, prepared to participate, that the meeting may not feel the leader's weakness. Encourage them in their efforts and make some timely suggestions to them. Pray for them, ask them to join with you in the prayer.

Q. Should unconverted persons be asked to lead the prayer meeting? Ans. No. How can those who do not pray themselves, who have no interest in prayer, and no faith in Him to whom prayer is offered, lead others in a prayer service?

Q. Should inexperienced leader ever give the invitation to stand up for prayer? Ans. If the leader is a thoroughly consecrated and earnest Christian, his plea might be helpful. But the possibility of an untimely application, or an inappropriate method, might be hurtful rather than beneficial to the meeting.

Q. Is it essential that there should be a different leader for each meeting? Ans. This is largely a question of the talent available in a leader. In some churches, even with a change of leaders, a person would not get a chance to lead beyond once or twice a year, while in smaller societies it would happen more frequently. If a leader has been instrumental in reviving interest in the meeting, don't change for the sake of change. Possibly it may be well to continue the same leader for two or three successive weeks, seldom longer.

Q. How can we develop spirituality in our prayer meetings? Ans. By encouraging much prayer as well as testimony.

These questions were selected from the many that were presented and answered by the writer at the prayer meeting conference in connection with the Baptist Young People's Union Convention, Toronto, July, 1894.

XX.
GENERAL SUGGESTIONS.

Prayer meetings can be better directed and more satisfactorily conducted, when they are not under the direct supervision and care of the pastor, by a committee consisting of two or more members.

The duties of the committee may be divided into five classes.

1. Topics and leaders.
2. Interest and attendance.
3. Ushers and ventilation.
4. Pauses.
5. Special programmes.

The duties mentioned are no doubt understood by simply calling attention to them, excepting, possibly, the second and fourth. The committee on interest and attendance should constantly be on the alert for such changes and suggestions as may improve the meetings. If the attendance is decreasing, the causes for it ought to be ascertained with the view to remedying them, or if the attendance is not sufficently large, efforts should be made by conference to find means of increasing it, if possible.

The committee on pauses, will arrange after a meeting in which several have occurred, to speak to five or six (selecting if possible, those not accustomed to taking part) and endeavor to pledge them to read a verse or take part in the first pause that occurs at the next meeting.

If we value the meeting for its great spiritual power, and look forward to it with the expectation of being benefited, our attitude going to and from the meeting will be in keeping with the service.

Much harm can be done the prayer meetings by outside criticism of the pastor or leader. In many cases after becoming familiar with the facts or reasons for much of the unkind comment and criticisms that are made, we find that there is little basis or foundation for them, the criticism arising often from a misapprehension or misunderstanding. The wisest course to pursue is to refrain from continuing conversations of this kind, unless to protect, if possible, the representatives of the church from being unjustly dealt with without their knowledge.

The success or failure of the prayer meetings depends to a large extent upon the encouragement or support given them by the individual members; and each of us, as dinividual Christians, should seek to exert an influence in the right direction.

The influence of the prayer meeting is not far reaching unless it encourages and helps the Christian to a daily cultivation of piety and godliness in the absence of the meeting. If it becomes a power to us in sustaining us amidst daily tempation and difficulty, it means something of vital importance to us and possibly to all.

If we find that other members of the church of our aquaintance are becoming careless, thoughtless or indifferent towards the prayer meeting, it becomes our duty and we should without hesitation use our best efforts and persuasion to get them to resume their place in the weekly gathering for prayer. Let us call on them, write them a kindly note, enlist others to aid us in securing again their co=operation and their presence.

With all the variations that may be suggested in way of leaders, topics, special music, and various other measures, there is yet one kind of meeting beside which all others are feeble in comparison, and that is where there are visible tokens of the Master's presence in the requests for prayer that are made for unconverted members of the family, friends or relatives; and where there are those that are inquiring "What shall I do to be saved?"

When there are evidences of interest of this kind, no chance should be lost in giving enquirers an opportunity to take the first step in acknowledging Christ and in pressing the Gospel claims of salvation before them.

Do not let the desire for well-regulated and properly conducted meetings stand in the way of an opportunity to lead a soul to Christ, which is of infinitely greater consequence.

Revival prayer meetings, judiciously conducted, add a vast deal of power to the church as well as to the regular prayer meetings.

There is a class of tramps who infest our large cities and go about begging for money, food, clothing or lodging, who never intend to do anything in return for what they receive. So there is also a large number of people who attend the prayer meetings weekly and recive all the benefit they can from what others have contributed, and never think of giving back anything of their own preparation in return. A fitting term for them, although perhaps a seemingly very harsh one, would be "prayer meeting cranks." Do not be one under any conditions. Do your duty regardless of the little satisfaction you may feel in its discharge. Who can tell what the results will be?

www.ingramcontent.com/pod-product-compliance
Lightning Source LLC
Chambersburg PA
CBHW020135170426
43199CB00010B/752